For the Love of Alabama

For the Love of Alabama

Journalism by Ron Casey and Bailey Thomson

Edited by Sam Hodges

With a Foreword
by Wayne Flynt

THE UNIVERSITY OF ALABAMA PRESS
Tuscaloosa

Typeface: Garamond

∞

The paper on which this book is printed meets the minimum requirements
of American National Standard for Information Sciences—Permanence of
Paper for Printed Library Materials, ANSI Z39.48-1984.

Library of Congress Cataloging-in-Publication Data

Casey, Ron (Ronald B.), 1951–2000.
For the love of Alabama : journalism by Ron Casey and Bailey Thomson /
edited by Sam Hodges ; with a foreword by Wayne Flynt.
p. cm
Includes index.
ISBN 978-0-8173-5666-8 (pbk. : alk. paper) 1. Alabama—Politics and
government—1951– I. Thomson, Bailey (Horace Bailey), 1949–2003.
II. Hodges, Sam (Samuel Lowe), 1955– III. Title.
F330.C37 2011
976.1—dc22

2010046561

Cover design by Todd Lape / Lape Designs

Publication is made possible in part through the generous support of the
Alabama Citizens for Constitutional Reform Foundation.

Contents

I. Fundamentals: The 1901 Alabama Constitution and State Taxes

II. Education and Children

III. Dixie's Broken Heart

IV. Race

V. Personal

Contents / vii

Foreword

The cliché that every cloud has a silver lining may be true. At least the lives of Ron Casey and Bailey Thomson provide strong evidence in favor of the silver lining theory.

The failure of generations of Alabama political leaders afforded both men sufficient storms. The wretched, wasteful, racist 1901 Constitution set the clouds gathering into a perfect storm. With that document as a club, selfish and self-serving economic elites ground down ordinary people into sharecropping and dead-end, low-wage, low-skill manufacturing jobs. Ordinary white people, wedded to traditionalism and fearful of change, allowed racism to separate them from blacks who labored in similar circumstances. Low taxes starved schools and public health which could have been avenues for their economic salvation.

By the 1980s Alabama rested on the bottom rung of a whole series of quality-of-life issues: infant mortality rates, life span, health, high school graduation rates, college graduates, per capita income, expenditure per schoolchild, teachers' salaries, just to name a few.

Worse than the condition was the apathy about the condition. Most politicians, beholden as they were to lobbyists for special interests, could be expected to ignore the storm clouds. Ministers were often too afraid of their congregations to even gaze at the horizon for fear of what they might see. Teachers and professors often were too preoccupied with their chores to scan the skies.

So it became the burden of reform-minded journalists to play Ezekiel and Jeremiah to Alabama's Jezebel and Zedekiah. Ron Casey and Bailey Thomson relished the role of prophet, partly because their religious faith encouraged it and partly because the sight of injustice caused their ethical juices to flow.

In Pulitzer Prize–winning and nominated editorials and series that remain highly relevant, they probed layer after layer of the storm bank: political corruption; denial of home rule; influence peddling; the inadequacies of the state constitution; lack of political and educational transparency and accountability. During years when most American newspapers were losing subscribers partly from pure boredom and the irrelevance of what they read, Alabamians were treated to the graceful prose and prophetic insights that Thomson and Casey broadcast across the pages of the *Mobile Press-Register* and the *Birmingham News*.

As practitioners of the "new journalism," they believed the issues of their times were too important to treat without passion and opinion. Though they solicited all views, they left no doubt about where they stood, or about their vision of a more just and progressive Alabama. And in their wake they left not merely words, but movements.

To some degree the stress of their calling and causes consumed them, taking their energy, time, and lives much too early. Both men loved their families, communities, traditions, and state. Indeed, that partly explains their compulsive determination to make Alabama better and their exhaustion in the cause. They were no less martyrs to the transcendent meaning of their ideals than were Reformation saints.

Thomson and Casey left many legacies: family and friends; movements and causes; reform structures; editorials; fragments of memoirs. That their good friend and fellow journalist Sam Hodges has gathered their writings as a living memorial to them and the state they loved is the good fortune of all Alabamians who now see more of the storm's hope and less of its darkness.

Wayne Flynt
Distinguished University Professor Emeritus
Auburn University

Acknowledgments

Editing this book has been a labor of love, one lightened considerably by many others. I must first thank my wife, Kit Lively, for her steadfast support and good counsel. Kristi Thomson is someone I've known for thirty years, from my days working for her husband, Bailey, on the editorial page of the *Shreveport Journal*. She immediately took to my idea for this book and was a consistently wise and encouraging sounding board. Her passion for state constitutional reform—and for a better quality of education for Alabama's children, particularly those who begin without advantages—honors the legacy of Bailey and Ron Casey. I first planned the book as a collection of Thomson pieces only, but when it struck me that pairing Thomson and Casey was a better way to go, Kristi agreed immediately—another example of her splendid character.

I didn't know Ron's wife, Margie Brooke, until undertaking this project. Getting to know her has been a pleasure, and I have appreciated her support. Ron Casey's older brother Buddy Casey generously spent a day with me, driving me around Midfield and introducing me to other family members.

Among *Mobile Press-Register* staff and alumni, I had encouragement and assistance from Mike Marshall, Dewey English, John Sledge, Sean Reilly, Roy Hoffman, and Carol McPhail. At the *Birmingham News,* Tom Scarritt, Bob Blalock, Joey Kennedy, and Mary Orndorff were very helpful contacts. Ed Mullins at The University of Alabama Department of Journalism was a friend to my efforts, as were other academicians with Alabama roots, notably John Northrop, Hardy Jackson, and Jerry Brown. I had important help from Bailey's great friend Stan Tiner, editor of the *Sun Herald* in Biloxi, Mississippi, as well as from Roy Peter Clark of The Poynter Institute. Danny Cusick, a former colleague of mine at the *Press-Register* and one of Bailey's first graduate students, helped considerably by reading an early draft and making comments. Susan Pace Hamill, of The University of Alabama Law School, not only cheered me on but facilitated the collection of some of these pieces with the help of certain "minions."

I'm sure, in the heat of deadline, I'm omitting some who should be mentioned by name. I'm also sure they'll forgive me, such generosity being typical of those who recognize the value of *For the Love of Alabama*.

Sam Hodges

For the Love of Alabama

Introduction

Ron Casey could have worked for bigger, more prestigious newspapers after leading the *Birmingham News* to one Pulitzer Prize for editorial writing in 1990 and the finals for another three years later. He stayed put, finding in his native Alabama a way of life that suited him and a passel of abiding social and governmental troubles that needed his pen.

Bailey Thomson left Alabama for newspaper jobs in Louisiana and Florida, but happily returned in his prime. Writing for the *Mobile Press-Register,* he was a Pulitzer finalist, and won the American Society of Newspaper Editors' top award for editorial writing. He would go on to teach journalism at The University of Alabama, using spare time and summers to write columns, editorial series, radio commentaries, speeches, and books. Always in the vanguard of technology as applied to journalism, he created an early Web site for his work. He called it simply "Alabama Writer."

Through the 1990s and a little beyond, Casey and Thomson documented their lover's quarrel with their state through scores of uncommonly well-researched, penetrating, and stylish editorials and columns. One could argue that they set the ongoing agenda for state constitution and tax reform. At the least, they pushed both efforts along, and meanwhile wrote many other pieces on state and local government, as well as personal essays. Both were mentors to young journalists, and both went beyond journalism to be leaders in organizations aimed at bettering their communities and state.

Casey died of a heart attack in 2000, at age forty-eight, moments after guest lecturing to a college journalism class. Thomson was shaken by his friend's death, and vowed to honor him by stepping up his own writing and organizing for reform of state government. Then in 2003, at age fifty-four, he too died of a heart attack, after overexerting himself in helping put out a neighbor's yard fire.

Following each death, tributes poured forth, including official ones from the state legislature, whose faults the writers had painstakingly committed to print. Over time, scholarships would be named for Casey and Thomson. There's a Bailey Thomson Award given by the Alabama Citizens for Constitutional Reform, an organization that Thomson helped start, and a Ron Casey building at Gateway, a Birmingham juvenile facility in which Casey took a journalistic and personal interest. Casey and Thomson were inducted posthumously, together, into The University of Alabama Communication Hall of Fame.

Few journalists get anywhere close to this much remembering. Still, there has remained a conspicuous omission—a book collecting what Casey and Thomson actually wrote about the state. Thus, *For the Love of Alabama.*

If it were a tribute volume only, the spirits of these writers would be disturbed. They wrote for change. *For the Love of Alabama* is nothing short of a primer on the state's intertwined, 1901 Constitution–grounded problems in government. While many of the politicians mentioned here have passed from the scene, the troubling realities they embodied have not. This book is today's news, not yesterday's. Yet there's considerable historical value to Thomson's and Casey's witness, since their pieces offer, cumulatively, perhaps the most vivid portrait yet of Alabama emerging from the George Wallace era. Finally, *For the Love of Alabama* merits publication because Casey and Thomson were—are—good company in print. They wrote clearly and feelingly about the things that mattered to them. One need not be invested in Alabama to respond to their prose, especially when it turns personal.

The writers were different in important ways.

Casey grew up in the blue-collar Birmingham suburb of Midfield, practically in the shadow of Woodward Iron Company, where his father began as a laborer and rose to superintendent of blast furnaces. The company provided not only jobs but housing and a doctor, and nearby Possum Creek "ran red" from pollution, his brother Buddy Casey recalled.

Thomson had a rural boyhood, in Aliceville, seat of west Alabama's Pickens County. His father ranked among the area's major cotton farmers, albeit using rented land. His mother's family relations included Fuller Kimbrell, a state finance director and legislator. Thomson grew up richly experiencing both farm and small-town life.

After earning his bachelor's degree in journalism, Casey worked twenty-seven years for the *Birmingham News,* rising quickly through the ranks and then settling in for his long tenure as editorial page editor. Practically all of his published writing was for that newspaper, in columns and unsigned editorials. (One of his former editorial page colleagues, Mary Orndorff, was asked how to know which of the unsigned editorials had been written by Casey, since the *News'* archives don't note authorship. "Easy. Just find the best ones," she said. "Ron wrote all of those.")

Thomson worked for newspapers in Tuscaloosa, Huntsville, Shreveport, Orlando, and Mobile. He spent a year at Stanford University on a journalism fellowship, and also earned a bachelor's degree, a master's degree in history, and a Ph.D. in journalism—all from The University of Alabama. He came late to full-time college teaching, but loved it, and quickly won not only tenure but a national award for journalism education. Apart from his newspaper work, he wrote for a range of scholarly and popular publications. He also wrote two books on Shreveport's history, and edited a collection of essays on the 1901 Alabama Constitution.

Casey was short, stocky, ruddy, bearded. He made fun of his pinched, nasal voice. Friends and family remember how smart he was—and how unpretentious. He was beloved by his staff for various reasons: his willingness to run interference for them over controversial editorials; his easing of deadline tension with wry remarks and parody awards; his gift not only for writing but editing. Colleague Joey Kennedy recalls that Casey would be apologetic about making changes to another journalist's writing ("If I messed it up, just change it back"), yet inevitably the line that prompted praise the next day would be the one Casey inserted.

Thomson was tall and broad, with a scholar's pallor. In serious conversation—his preferred kind—he would fix the other person with a rational stare, rarely nodding or doing anything else to jolly things along. He demanded much of students and underlings, but much more of himself. By hard work, not from any facility for foreign languages, he became fluent in Spanish. He was a rigorous journal keeper, and assembled a formidable archive of his journalism career: letters, notes, drafts. Part of his chronic restlessness owed to trying to decide which hard project to undertake next.

More striking than Casey's and Thomson's differences were the many traits they had in common.

Both knew their luck in having had parents who were readers and who talked about ideas and current events, especially politics, at the dinner table. Both became serious readers themselves, and decided early to become writers.

Casey and Thomson came of age as Alabama made its tortured way from segregation to integration, and they spent their college years at one of the civil rights battlegrounds—The University of Alabama. They arrived not long after George Wallace stood in the schoolhouse door, and they were observers, participants, and recorders (for the college newspaper, the *Crimson White*) as the campus underwent profound social change.

As the years went on, Thomson and Casey deepened their understanding of Alabama through careful study of its history. After Thomson got his master's in history, he wrote articles for the state's historical journal, the *Alabama Review*. Casey proceeded less formally, but colleagues recall that his copy of Malcolm McMillan's *Constitutional Development in Alabama, 1798–1901* was as underlined as a country preacher's Bible, and that his idea of beach reading was any serious book about Alabama.

Casey and Thomson shared a belief that Alabama's 1901 Constitution was the root of the state's underachievement in so many areas: education, health care, environmental protection, women's and children's issues, and basic competence of state and local government. They advocated what might be called pragmatic progressivism, including constitutional reform, a fairer state tax system, more local autonomy and overall transparency in government, stronger support for public schools, and an owning up to the state's racial history. Each argued, in piece after piece, that the people of Alabama were better than their leaders. They wrote admiringly of the civil rights movement, and of white Alabamians who'd gone against the grain, such as Judge Frank Johnson and Clarence Cason.

Neither Casey nor Thomson fit the stereotype of the cynical, flask-in-drawer journalist. They matured into dedicated family men, and both were serious Bible students, with Casey deeply involved in his United Methodist church. Each risked overstepping the boundaries of journalism—by becoming part of a Leadership Alabama class, and by joining reform organizations.

Their friendship deepened in their last years, and one question they entertained together was how involved they should be, beyond writing, in working for change. Thomson, in a tribute written just after Casey's death, recalled asking for advice about whether he should be part of creating what would become Alabama Citizens for Constitutional Reform. Casey's answer was typically straightforward, and gave no weight to convention or appearances. "Just do what you think is right," Casey said.

This book is organized by themes, beginning with the state constitution and taxes, moving on to education and children, and then to a section called "Dixie's Broken Heart," about the inadequacies of the Alabama state government and the related problem of special-interest influence. There is, inevitably, a group of essays on race. A sampling of Casey's and Thomson's personal essays comes next. Thomson's extended memoir, "A Queen for King Cotton," about his family's experiment with raising sheep—and, by extension, the twilight of agriculture as a dominant force in the state—concludes the book. There are more individual pieces by Casey. Thomson, who wrote in longer forms, has a slight edge in word count.

Along the way, readers will encounter such standouts as Casey's "The Cricket's Song," from the Pulitzer Prize–winning series on Alabama's tax system, and Thomson's recounting of the obscure but telling life of Jackson Giles, a freedman who conscientiously voted for years, then lost that right to the 1901 Alabama Constitution. Throughout *For the Love of Alabama,* worthy subjects receive their due from two accomplished writers on a mission to understand and improve their state.

Casey once said, "If you want to sip wine, go to France. If you want to write editorials, go to Alabama."

At the risk of mixing images, here, in the form of editorials and more, is some mighty fine wine.

Sam Hodges

I

Fundamentals: The 1901 Alabama Constitution and State Taxes

Bailey Thomson and Ron Casey did the reading and reporting necessary to know how the Alabama Constitution of 1901 came to be and what its consequences have been—including its effects on state taxes. They made the constitution and taxes subjects for award-winning editorial series as well as for daily editorials and columns.

It seems fair—modest, really—to assert that their writings on the constitution and tax reform educated many across the state and forced top politicians to take stands.

Here are some of their best pieces on these themes.

RON CASEY

We, the People

May 9, 1993, *Birmingham News,* unsigned editorial

The Alabama Constitution of 1901 begins, "We, the people of the state of Alabama . . ."

But that is a lie. It was written by 155 white males and approved by 108,613 voters in a state with a population of 1.8 million.

It's an awful document, written with three immoral aims: to deny the vote to black citizens; to make sure property taxes would remain minimal for the timber, agricultural, and iron industries that ruled the state; and to ensure that very little could happen in Alabama unless it first was approved by the state legislature those interests controlled.

Even many of the people who wrote it never expected it to last more than twenty or thirty years. Yet it has, through attempt after attempt to change it.

Now there is another one in the works. Senator Mac Parsons of Hueytown last week maneuvered a proposal through the state senate which would allow Alabamians to vote on whether they would like to see a constitutional convention held in 1995.

Maybe it's a fluke. Maybe no one was watching. Nonetheless, it's a live wire.

This outmoded constitution must be dealt with. Constitutions are supposed to be blueprints for how orderly change may occur in a society. Ours is an attempt to stop change in its tracks.

It has been amended 550 times because it is impossible for modern government to function under its auspices.

Every time we have an election in this state, Alabama voters dutifully try to wade through a slew of Byzantine amendments.

Decatur wants to set up an elected board of education. Amend the constitution. Jefferson County wants to simplify how it licenses real estate agents. Amend the constitution. Marion County wants to set up a public water authority. Amend the basic document of state government.

Ours is not a constitution that talks about fundamental rights and principles of government, as does the U.S. Constitution. It is a code of often conflicting laws set in constitutional concrete to make it difficult to alter them.

Section 96, for example, says no court fee shall be set for one county that does not apply to all. But over one hundred exemptions have been granted to that, and there are only sixty-seven counties in the state. There is no article which specifically speaks to county government, yet there are more than 350 laws in this state dealing with county finances.

There are dangers in trying to fix our constitution's shortcomings through a convention. Delegates would be elected from the 105 state House districts, with six each selected from our seven congressional districts and four elected statewide.

They would not be able to take away fundamental rights guaranteed by the U.S. Constitution. But if they end up more interested in representing special interests than representing the people, they could do great harm.

But there is also hope that voter rolls truly reflecting the people of Alabama would produce a convention representative of the state; that community leaders not normally willing to make the commitment a four-year term of office might require would be more interested in running for a chance to rewrite the constitution; that the state's economic interests are so much more diverse now than in 1901 that no pack of special interests would be able to monopolize the outcome.

Every other Southern state that adopted a segregationist constitution at the turn of the century has gone back to rewrite it. Alabama should, too. Though we must not go about it flippantly. The House should seriously consider if this is the best route available.

What can be done to make sure the eventual product of a constitutional revision is a highly principled, not politically partisan, document of which the people of Alabama will be proud? To make sure revision is not accompanied by an explosion of lawsuits testing alterations?

This is a tough problem, but we can be comforted by one fact: we could hardly do worse than the callous, unwieldy, exploitive document of 1901.

BAILEY THOMSON

When the Lights Dimmed

October 15, 2000, *Mobile Press-Register,*
from "Century of Shame" series

Jackson W. Giles knew Alabama had changed, but the fury of the new order shocked him. Musty court records at the state's archives tell how he lost his right to vote in Alabama in only a day, and why he never got it back.

Mr. Giles had voted for twenty years and had been active in Montgomery's Fourth Ward. But like other men, he had to register under the rigid voting laws of Alabama's new constitution of 1901.

The stiff qualifications didn't deter him. Mr. Giles had a good job at the post office. He could read and write. He and his wife, Mary, owned their home, and he had paid his poll tax of $1.50.

But Mr. Giles was black, and he had to satisfy three white registrars that Thursday, March 13, 1902. And they turned him away, as they did thousands of other African Americans who sought to sign up that year—among them a Methodist bishop.

Meanwhile, no white applicant left the Montgomery courthouse—at least during 1902—without being a voter, the old records show.

As Mr. Giles and other blacks had feared, the democratic lights were dimming across Alabama. The *Montgomery Advertiser* of the day explained, "It was generally understood that the spirit of the new constitution would be carried out and the Negro barred from participating in the future government of the state."

By 1908, only two percent of black men in Alabama could vote, a stark reversal of African Americans' enfranchisement after the Civil War.

The new constitution had done its job effectively, but it hadn't stopped there. Indeed, it wasn't supposed to stop.

Whites who had the misfortune to be poor became snared in Alabama's new punitive laws and lost their rights, as well. In time, the number of disfranchised whites exceeded that of blacks who had lost the vote.

In the decade before 1901, nearly eighty percent of eligible Alabamians, white and black, voted. By 1940, only about a third of adults were even registered to vote.

The document that did this wicked work, the 1901 state constitution, remains Alabama's fundamental charter, the malicious child of a coalition of big planters and industrial magnates. Through fraud, these bosses enshrined their rule in the state's organic law and eliminated their political enemies.

Alabamians have yet to reverse this century of shame, though we keep amending the decrepit 1901 document. The fathers of this deed have gone to dust, but their sins haunt the living.

Jackson W. Giles became less than a full man under the law because the state's reactionary political bosses were determined to strangle dissent and perpetuate their power. They had been frightened by the turbulence of the 1890s, when hard times stalked the land. A coalition of small farmers and workers, white and black, had risen to demand reforms.

This Populist movement insisted on fair labor laws. It opposed leasing convicts to mines and sawmills—a brutal industrial slavery that competed with free workers. And the Populists wanted honest elections. They were tired of the bosses winning statewide contests by stuffing boxes in the vast plantation region known as the Black Belt, which girdled the state's middle.

The champion of these reformers was Reuben F. Kolb, a former commissioner of agriculture. In some places, his supporters joined callused hands across the racial line, which frightened the bosses. Twice, in 1892 and 1894, Mr. Kolb apparently won the governorship—only to have his victories nullified by fraudulent votes in the Black Belt, according to the state's historians. To protest, Kolb's backers held their own shadow inauguration in Montgomery on December 1, 1894.

In response to such challenges, conservative forces began agitating for a new state constitution to replace the 1875 version, which allowed all men to vote. Their cry became "white supremacy."

Opportunity arrived when the bosses tightened their control of state government with the election of 1900. They called for a referendum on whether to summon a constitutional convention. In counties where Populist discontent simmered, yeoman farmers smelled a conspiracy. Many stayed away from the polls.

The bosses got their convention the same way they had destroyed Mr. Kolb: through a fraudulent vote count in the Black Belt, where an African American majority labored under the planters' domination. Since the waning of Reconstruction in 1874, planters in that region had refined their vote-stealing into an art. They would throw out thousands of legitimate ballots and substitute fakes—"counting in and counting out," they called it.

The convention began at noon on Tuesday, May 21, 1901, when 155 delegates, all white and all male, assembled in the state House of Representatives. Montgomery's skies cleared, and the temperature rose into the seventies, inviting spectators to fill the galleries. The delegates elected as their president John B. Knox of Anniston, who was said to be the state's highest-paid corporate lawyer.

The next day, Mr. Knox announced the ruling Democrats' intention to disfranchise African Americans, who a generation earlier had stepped up from bondage to citizenship. "There is in the white man an inherited capacity for government, which is wholly wanting in the Negro," bellowed Mr. Knox. After hearing dissent from a minority of delegates, the convention followed Mr. Knox's lead and drew up the most restrictive voting rules it could muster against blacks. One effective method gave registrars discretion to determine whether an applicant was of "good character" and thereby worthy of voting.

But the conspirators had another, quieter motive: they wanted to remove as many poor white voters as they could, thereby reducing the chance of another Populist revolt. In asking for a convention, the bosses had promised that no white man would lose his vote. (Of course, they never considered women to be worthy of suffrage and refused to grant them rights.) The fine print in the proposed new constitution, however, called for registering white males during a one-year grace period—then slamming the door shut with stringent literacy and property-holding requirements.

Their new document included another particularly sharp weapon: the poll tax. To be eligible to register, a citizen first had to pay $1.50 each year. Many families didn't have that much left over in a week or even a month. Worse, if a voter missed paying for any year, he had to pay the back taxes, too, up to $36.

Apart from the new voting rules, however, the framers largely readopted the themes of the state's 1875 constitution, pampering their benefactors with low taxes and expressing such distrust of local government that counties received no power to pass laws.

With their work finished, the framers turned to winning ratification in the face of widespread opposition, particularly in the heavily white counties of Alabama's northern hill country and the rolling wiregrass region in the southeast.

The *Montgomery Advertiser,* mouthpiece for the reactionaries, let slip the framers' plan for victory when it declared that the Black Belt "will roll up one of those old-time Democratic majorities for the new Constitution." In other words, they intended to steal it.

Returns were late arriving on November 11, 1901, but slowly the great deceit unfolded. The planters had outdone themselves: if we are to believe the results, the "yes" vote was more than ninety-five percent in six Black Belt counties where African Americans accounted for seventy-five percent of the population.

Elsewhere, the new constitution lost—76,263 to 72,389—in what was, no doubt, an accurate reflection of the majority's will.

Despite the certainty of fraud, Gov. William D. Jelks certified the new constitution on November 21, 1901.

Four months later, Jackson W. Giles was busy fighting back.

Black opponents of the new constitution had promised that legal challengers would emerge. Mr. Giles was one of those challengers. After organizing the Colored Man's Suffrage Association in Montgomery, he became the plaintiff in a series of lawsuits later known as the "Alabama Cases."

The first stop was a lawsuit against the three white registrars in the city court of Montgomery, presided over by Judge A. D. Sayre. Predictably, Mr. Sayre had no sympathy. The judge was the epitome of the Black Belt aristocrat, as his son-in-law, novelist F. Scott Fitzgerald, later wrote.

So began the appeals that took Mr. Giles all the way to the U.S. Supreme Court, where his counsel, Wilford H. Smith, became the first black lawyer to argue a case before the justices. Mr. Smith informed them that Montgomery County registrars had refused to enroll more than five thousand black voters solely because of their race, in violation of the Fourteenth and Fifteenth Amendments of the U.S. Constitution. As evidence of foul intent, he introduced the vitriolic speeches of Mr. Knox and other leaders of the 1901 convention.

But the high court's justices, influenced perhaps by a rising tide of racism nationwide, rejected the plea. The majority declined to act on what Chief Justice Oliver Wendell Holmes Jr. dismissed as a political question.

As democracy's lights flickered, Mr. Giles drifted into obscurity. He and several other black men lost their jobs at the Montgomery post office. The 1904 city directory shows Mr. Giles living above a small grocery store at 120 South Highland, a short street less than a mile from the Alabama capitol. Records in the state archives fall silent about him soon after that date.

Nearly a century later, the tragic chapter that Mr. Giles saw open in 1901 has yet to close, although the federal government gradually guaranteed suffrage for all—first to women, in 1920 with the Nineteenth Amendment; then to blacks, in 1965 with the Voting Rights Act; and finally to poor people in general in 1966, when the U.S. Supreme Court struck down the poll tax.

The persistence of the 1901 constitution, spiked as it is with antiquated provisions and contemptible notions, demonstrates that Alabamians have yet to show much genius for self-government—or justice, for that matter.

Yet the renewed flame of democracy beckons. More people than ever sense the possibilities for writing a new state constitution. Rallies in cities such as Huntsville, Tuscaloosa, Jacksonville, and soon in Mobile demonstrate reform is on the public's agenda. These aroused citizens want not only to atone for past sins, but also to brighten every corner for the future.

RON CASEY

The Bubbling Caldron

August 26, 1990, *Birmingham News,* from Pulitzer Prize–
winning "What They Won't Tell You about Your Taxes" series

The first thing they won't tell you about your taxes concerns the caldron of poverty, exploitation, and rotten politics from which they bubbled.

Outgrowths of our thorny history still hold us back. They germinate in the
uprootings of farm families from the fields to the smokestacks after the close of
the Civil War.

Auburn University history professor Dr. Wayne Flynt and other historians
have outlined a long, slow slide into deprivation.

Many were on the precipice of poverty before the war began. Four years of
missing manpower, bad crops, and destruction pushed them over the edge.

Thousands lost their land. More than eighty-five percent of the state's white
residents owned property before the war. Over the decades, that figure continued to fall, until by 1930 sixty-five percent of Alabama's farmers had to farm soil
owned by someone else.

The landless blacks and whites searched for something better than tenant
farming or the cyclical bondage of sharecropping.

Lumber became a major industry here and around the Southeast after timber companies used and abused homestead laws to gain control of thousands of
acres of federal lands. Textile mills, coal mines, and blast furnaces grew up in
the foreground of a rural landscape.

Near the turn of the century, former subsistence farmers could make a dollar a day at a sawmill; earn $3 for a week of twelve-hour days in a textile plant;
or even earn fifty cents for every ton of coal scratched from some of the most
dangerous mines in the country. Alabama miners died on the average of ten per
month between 1900 and 1910.

Instead of helping the struggling, our legislature went in another direction. In 1888, for instance, a five-year tax exemption for small family farmers was turned down. But state tax laws were revised that same year to help big planters.

Following Mississippi, South Carolina, Louisiana, and North Carolina, in 1901 Alabama adopted a new constitution aimed at barring blacks from voting. But its insidious features, like the cumulative poll tax due weeks ahead of an election, kept low-income whites away from the ballot box also.

The year 1901 marked another milestone. It was the last time the Alabama legislature altered its representation for more than sixty years.

Instead of redrawing its House and senate districts based on the state's population after each census, the legislature stood still. No matter what shifts in population took place, the same counties got the same number of lawmakers.

In 1960, Jefferson County had a population of 634,864. Yet it had one senator, just like 12,917-person Lowndes County.

Control of state government remained in the hands of the big-planter counties in the Black Belt in collusion with unscrupulous industrialists.

Though most of the state's residents, wealth, and revenues were supplied by north Alabama, the Black Belt's grip remained in place until federal courts ordered redistricting in the early 1960s.

The Great Depression devastated Alabama. Employment plummeted here like nowhere else in the South. In 1935, Franklin Roosevelt called Birmingham "the worst hit town in the country."

Even with so many strikes against it, Alabama was on the verge of making a comeback after World War II. Federal dollars and federal jobs poured in. Alabama lured new industries with tax incentives and the promise of cheap labor.

But by the 1960s, the state was embroiled in one racial confrontation after another as the walls of segregation fell and the doors to the voting booths opened. The turmoil ended an abhorrent system, but it also spawned continuing damage to the state's ability to lure out-of-state businesses.

The federal money began drying up in the 1970s and 1980s, and the economy turned global. Textile jobs went to even cheaper labor in the Far East. Coal came pouring in from South America. Steel jobs went to Japan.

With an undereducated work force, bargain-basement services, and a reputation for racial turmoil, Alabama withered in the shadows of Sun Belt growth.

One 1984 estimate said that as many as twenty-five percent of its people could qualify for food stamps.

The political diseases of the hard-scrabble years plague us still:

• We live in a state with no tradition of strong financial support for public education. The children went to work.

In 1900, 59 percent of Alabama's boys and 31.4 percent of her girls between the ages of ten and fifteen held a job. By 1910 the percentages increased to 61.9 percent and 41.3 percent.

Many mills, mines, and factories calculated pay on "family wages," or how much more to pay for new sons and daughters at the plant.

The poor saw little value in a high school or college education. That attitude passed from one generation to the next. In the 1980 census, 43.5 percent of Alabama's people above the age of twenty-five did not have a high school diploma.

Alabama ranked fifty-first in the nation in state and local revenue per person for schools in a 1987 census update.

- We live in a state where the people have a gut-level distrust of their government. Demagoguery has been more in vogue than democracy; corruption more prevalent than compassion.

  Yet the structures erected to guard against abuse of the public trust hamstring our elected officials. So much of the state's money is locked into outdated earmarking systems, we can't make revenues match needs. We can't deal with debilitating problems.

- We live in a state where officials have paid more attention to protecting big-land interests than people.

  For decades, we have bent over backward to make sure the large landholders, timber companies, and corporate land barons who controlled Montgomery paid next to nothing in taxes.

- We live in a state where the poor, black and white, who were kept away from the ballot box for decades have seen a shamefully unfair burden of taxes laid on their backs.

Little wonder they don't want you to know about the tax system which bubbled up from such a vile brew.

BAILEY THOMSON

Blessed Are the Privileged

October 17, 2000, *Mobile Press-Register,*
from "Century of Shame" series

Alabama's constitution is silent about equal protection for citizens. But don't assume that everyone is treated alike—especially when it comes to taxes. Consider the following two cases from Mobile County:

Buchanan Lumber Company specializes in hardwood, mostly for the wholesale trade. Bill Buchanan moved to Mobile in 1965, when he and his two brothers bought the company.

The company, which has thirteen acres near the Alabama State Docks, used to employ 115 workers when it ran a sawmill and supplied furniture-makers in the Carolinas. But demand dried up, forcing Buchanan Lumber to find other customers, many of them overseas. Now, its Mobile work force is down to twenty-five people, although the company continues to expand elsewhere, most recently with a sawmill at Aliceville, west of Tuscaloosa.

Through good times and bad, the company has paid its taxes. This year, according to records in the county Revenue Commissioner's Office, the property tax bill amounted to $5,876 on just the thirteen acres in Mobile. The tax office values the land, excluding its buildings and machinery, at $570,500.

Across town, according to revenue records, another parcel of land is appraised for taxes at almost the same figure—$570,000. But the comparison ends there. And so does the tax fairness.

A company listed in the records as C G Investment Venture paid just $38 in property taxes this year on this nineteen-acre tract at Grelot and Cody roads in sprawling west Mobile.

Why does speculative property in the city's booming suburbs virtually escape taxation, while land in a family business, in an older area, bears the full rate?

The answer is simple: Fairness disappeared twenty years ago under Amendment 373 to the state's constitution. The Alabama Farmers Federation, known as Alfa, which speaks for some of the state's wealthiest landowners, panicked legislators and voters into approving what amounts to a tax subsidy. People feared that honest appraisal of property in Alabama, which the federal courts had ordered to replace wildly disparate valuations, would invite confiscation.

The legislature could have calmed such fears by appraising all property for tax purposes at the actual value, effectively broadening the tax base. Legislators then could have lowered rates for all owners, while allowing specific relief for certain hardship cases, such as elderly people on low, fixed incomes. And legislators could have protected farmers and timber-growers in urban counties from rising values, thereby preserving green spaces around cities, by following the lead of states that appraise such property as if it sat in rural areas, rather than next to a shopping center or a subdivision.

Alabama's legislature may have been interested in all these sensible ideas, but not for long. Instead, legislators went along with Alfa and Gov. George Wallace to gut the state's capacity to levy fair property taxes.

First, Amendment 373 required that business property be assessed for taxes at twice the rate of residential or agricultural property. (Property belonging to utilities is assessed at three times the rate.) Next, the amendment reduced the already low tax bite on agricultural land by as much as half or more. It did this through a unique and arbitrary trick known as "current use."

Alabama applies current use to virtually any property, urban or rural, where owners claim to be growing something for sale. The tract may be a paper company's vast pine plantation miles from the nearest town. Or it may be a few acres next to a mall where a speculator has stuck some pine trees.

Indeed, more than half the property on Mobile County's tax rolls has current use protection. As a result, the land in this category produces just one percent of the county's property taxes. Taxed at its fair market value, the land would yield $2.4 million in annual county taxes; taxed under current use, it yields $1.3 million, according to the county revenue office.

This rip-off is particularly outrageous because speculators can sit on expensive urban property and pay next to nothing in taxes. Records at the courthouse show that C G Investment Venture put the pine-covered tract at Cody and Grelot roads—an area fast building up with houses and apartments—under current use in 1982.

The Mobile County tax office, like others around the state, usually doesn't question an owner's request for such status so long as timber or hay is present.

In such cases, the law requires that Freda Roberts, Mobile County's revenue commissioner, ignore the property's actual use in levying taxes. Instead, she must apply an arcane formula that Alfa helped devise. This formula is supposed to reflect the productive value of the land, but its main function is to prevent fair taxation. Under this arbitrary rule, the nineteen-acre tract is valued at just $387 per acre for taxes, though it is prime for development.

(Imagine such a tract situated in the boondocks of Mobile County, far from any development. On the market, it would be worth, on average, $804 per acre for the bare land alone. That figure comes from a recent report, prepared by the Extension Service at Auburn University, on comparative land values in Alabama.)

In addition to current use, the constitution limits taxation of agricultural land to ten percent of its assessed value. So this crazy math further reduces the taxable value of the Cody and Grelot tract to $39 per acre. When the county multiplies that figure by the tax rate within the city limits, which is 0.00515, the tax bill is $2 per acre—or $38 for the nineteen acres.

C G Investment Venture sold the property on June 30 to another company, Arlington Park Apartments, which plans an apartment complex there. The price was $912,871—or $48,046 per acre.

Apologists for current use excuse such abuse of the tax system by pointing to a provision in the law that penalizes owners when they sell land for purposes other than agriculture. The assessor can apply the full tax rate to the property for the present year and two previous years.

But sellers typically just pass the extra taxes on for the new owners to pay, or tack the amount to the selling price. Meanwhile, they keep the subsidies from all those previous years when their property qualified for current use.

What a deal. In fact, tax experts say no other state treats its big landowners so tenderly as does Alabama. Nor does any other state follow Alabama in confusing legitimate protection of farmland with blatant favoritism.

This favoritism becomes apparent when one weighs the equity of Alabama's property tax system against that of its neighbors.

Mississippi, for example, generally has low tax rates, and protects farmland and timberland, too. But a simple comparison of tax bills along the Alabama-Mississippi border suggests that Mississippi landowners carry a fairer share of the tax burden in their state.

Take the case of Sustainable Forests, a company in Chatom, fifty miles north of Mobile. It owns a tract of timberland that flows from Mobile County into George County, Mississippi. On the Alabama side, there are 309 acres; on the Mississippi side, 246 acres.

Sustainable Forests paid $4.18 per acre in taxes on its Mississippi timberland for 1999, according to George County records.

But in Alabama, where the land qualifies for current use, Sustainable Forests paid $1.67 per acre, Mobile County records show. Both states tax only the land and not the timber.

Even before Amendment 373, Alabama's 1901 constitution starved public services by imposing miserly limits on property taxes. This condition led the Brookings Institution to conclude in 1932 that the constitution had created a "warped and distorted" tax system that tried to substitute a confusing jumble for fair property taxes.

Today, the Alabama Constitution continues to play favorites through clever schemes that protect privileged landowners. What this obsolete document can't do, however, is hide the folly of pampering timber corporations, speculators, and other wealthy interests at the expense of public schoolchildren and poor families.

RON CASEY

Harnessing the Tempest

September 1, 1990, *Birmingham News,*
from Pulitzer Prize–winning "What They
Won't Tell You about Your Taxes" series

If you want to stir up a tempest, disturb the pocketbooks of the powerful.

Nothing creates more commotion in Montgomery than altering taxes.

That's why substantial changes in Alabama's tax system have come only after great crises: the collapse of the state bank in the 1830s; the Civil War and Reconstruction; the Great Depression.

This summer a small group set up by the legislature is quietly plotting the course of a peaceful revolution. The Tax Reform Study Commission will make its report next January as the next governor and legislature take office.

Its report could simply gather dust on a shelf, as have so many others. But it has a genuine chance of inspiring major change for a variety of reasons.

Foremost among them is that our taxes no longer fit our state. The structure is designed to nourish an economy heavily dependent on agriculture for jobs and dollars.

So many of the dozens of pages of tax breaks in our sales tax subsidize agriculture. Property taxes on farm-, timber-, and pastureland under "current use" classification are ridiculously low.

Agriculture is still a vital industry. But it offers our people fewer and fewer opportunities. Between 1950 and 1960 alone, the number of farm jobs in this state declined by sixty-one percent. The Southern Regional Education Board predicts that by 2000, twenty-four percent of those jobs remaining will be gone.

Our tax system endures not because of logic, but because of the political muscle flexed by those who set it up and the complexity of the systems they fashioned to lock it into place.

You can't substantially change our property taxes without amending the Alabama Constitution, the basic foundation of state government. That takes a three-fifths vote of each house of the legislature, and then approval of Alabama's voters.

You can't raise the income tax without amending the constitution. You can't significantly alter the Byzantine system of earmarking without amending the constitution. Even something as mundane as a franchise tax on business is mandated by the constitution.

What if the founding fathers two hundred years ago had not only outlined the form of our federal government, but also detailed a tax code?

The balance of power is shifting. Where once the farm belt and the "Big Mule" industrialists ruled the state with little interference, today's "Big Mules"— if corporate leaders can be called that—are in favor of a major tax reform effort.

The Alabama Business Council has led the charge. During the last legislative session, it proposed a blue-ribbon panel to study taxes in the midst of a dispute about the corporate franchise tax.

Even when the dispute was settled, the council continued the strong lobbying that eventually led to the Tax Reform Study Commission's creation.

The political strength of the big-land interests is on the decline. The loss of perennial supporters like Earl Goodwin and Rick Manley in the senate in the last legislative sessions is a continuation of the slow relaxation of their grip.

Instead of stonewalling any change in property taxes, those interests would do well to accept a fair tax, one in line with what others in the region assess.

"The bigger they come, the harder they fall" also applies to taxation.

Take the case of the toxic waste industry. For years, dumpers blocked anything more than a pittance tax on hazardous waste buried in Alabama. As the public became more aware of that minimal burden, and more resentful of it, taxes were jacked up—from $1 a ton to $112 a ton for out-of-state dumpers.

A similar backlash could occur on timberland taxes.

Property taxes are the key to tax reform. As long as giant agribusiness, timber, and corporate acreages escape anything approaching a fair share, no other interest group will accept tax changes without a knock-down, drag-out fight.

This commission is the best vehicle to drive reasonable change. In the past, tax reform studies have come from academics, or members of some blue-ribbon panel of experts (and allies) appointed by the governor. They could not form a consensus the breadth of Alabama's economic interests might rally around.

This commission's membership includes representatives of farming and timber, labor, academia, business, law, and politics. Its report, after months of testimony and public meetings around the state, should be a broad-based assessment of what Alabama needs.

It can add to the chances of success by following two simple rules: be fair and be clear.

It has to propose something more than just a series of convenient tax hikes. Louisiana governor Buddy Roemer tried that kind of "tax reform" a couple of years ago. His package would have made $600 million in temporary taxes, mostly sales taxes, permanent. It was clobbered by Louisiana voters.

Nor can tax reform be sold with games, the most prevalent of which is the voter-pleasing notion that overhauling Alabama's system should be "revenue neutral."

Anyone who talks about revenue-neutral tax reform here is talking about less money for schools. The most critical problem is the state's always bankrupt General Fund. The only way to fix that without raising more revenue is to take money away from education.

We need more revenue, and we can provide it. Alabama only makes about eighty-seven percent of the tax effort of the average state system, according to the latest census figures.

Tax reform has to be clear. When this commission makes its final report, it should be in crystal-clear language, with precise suggestions any Alabama taxpayer can understand.

And it ought to offer a bill, ready to be introduced in the legislature, based on its recommendations. Then the people can see which of their elected representatives want to do more than just give lip service to tax reform.

Give the people the plain truth and they will harness the tempest's energy for progress.

BAILEY THOMSON

Hogs at the Door

October 12, 1998, *Mobile Press-Register,*
from "Dixie's Broken Heart" series

Ray and Barbara Stevens had only $76 when they married, but they vowed to own a farm one day. They worked, saved, and eventually bought and cleared 250 acres in St. Clair County, where they raise cattle and operate a wrecker service at Ashville. They built a brick home and added a swimming pool.

Then in 1991, the Stevenses' dream collapsed. A neighbor moved about five thousand hogs next to their property. The family has lived with a nauseating odor ever since. "We can't even raise our windows," says Ray Stevens. "We can't hang clothes on the line." When their granddaughter, who is now thirteen, visits, she often won't go out and swim because of the stinky air.

St. Clair has four such hog farms now, and dozens more may be on the way as big corporations transform pig parlors into pork factories. Thousands of animals packed tightly together produce the equivalent of a small city's waste. But the stuff doesn't go into a sewage system. It flows into open pits, which belch odoriferous clouds that may drift for miles. Even worse, these waste pits can break under a heavy rain, fouling streams and lakes with pollution.

Such disasters have inspired tougher laws elsewhere. So now more corporate operators are moving quietly into Alabama. Our state doesn't control animal waste unless farms channel it into public waters. Regulators won't restrict a corporate farm just because neighbors such as the Stevenses don't like it.

In St. Clair and other targeted counties, people beg for help. Can't local officials stop this threat? That's why people elected them, isn't it—to protect the health and property of decent, hardworking folks?

Yes, but here's the catch: Alabama's state constitution denies counties the right to govern and tax themselves. Instead of "home rule," Alabamians have despotism from Montgomery, which forces local leaders to ask the legislature for authority to do virtually anything. That's why forty percent of legislative business concerns local matters.

As a result, counties can't control nuisances, even when they may threaten citizens' health. Only three counties have even limited zoning power to guide development in rural areas, where about half of Alabama's growth is occurring. There's little to stop a hog farm, a junkyard, a racetrack, or some other objectionable business from elbowing into a residential area.

But the absurdity doesn't stop with land use. Consider these typical cases:

Residents in Mobile County's Twin Lakes subdivision watch their yards turn into ponds during heavy rains as runoff from nearby parking lots and other development floods in. But the county can't require adequate drainage for new businesses and homes.

Tuscaloosa County now has its deeds in a computer database. Title companies, lawyers, and others are willing to pay for online access to that information. The revenue could help pay the courthouse bills. But the county clerk can't sell that access because the legislature hasn't authorized the service.

About three thousand people are moving to Blount County every year. Development is gobbling up farmland, swamping schools with new students, and packing roads with traffic. It's only fair that this growth pay for the services it requires. But Alabama doesn't give county officials the tools they need to raise adequate revenue.

Why does Alabama hamstring its counties when neighboring states consider government closest to the people to be the most effective? One reason is that special interests such as the Alabama Farmers Federation, "Alfa" for short, lobby hard with generous campaign contributions to keep home rule out of the state's constitution. These special interests resist reasonable rules for land use so they can do as they please, right down to building a hog farm across the road from a home.

These same interests and their legislative toadies make sure local governments can't impose fair taxation. Result? Owners of agricultural and timberland pay the nation's lowest property tax rates.

Alabama is asking for more messy problems unless citizens demand the right to home rule.

Just such an uprising happened in South Carolina in the early 1970s, when local people changed their state constitution to allow self-government. Before that reform happened, South Carolina's local laws were even more backward, if that's possible, than those of Alabama. In a typical case, the local legislative delegation supervised its county's affairs. These legislators even wrote the local budgets and approved them in the state capitol.

But in 1973, reformers managed to put the issue of home rule to a vote of the people. This event occurred after a commission worked to overhaul the state's constitution, which was as antiquated as Alabama's present document. Overwhelmingly, citizens said they wanted stronger local government; thus, a more democratic era began.

New voting laws made this transition to home rule even more necessary. Legislative districts began to cross county lines to ensure fair representation. That districting change meant a legislator might not know enough or care enough about a county's affairs to make wise decisions. All the more reason, then, to give local people the right to govern themselves.

Home rule restricts legislators to passing laws that affect the entire state. They can no longer single out a community or county for special action.

Naturally, South Carolina's legislators resisted giving up their local power, and they still find ways to meddle, especially on taxes. But because reformers persisted, county and municipal governments now can manage their communities' growth and provide services their people need.

Indeed, home rule came just in time. South Carolina is the country's tenth-fastest-growing state. As in Alabama, most of the growth occurs in urban counties, such as Spartanburg along Interstate 85. There, a traveler passing the giant BMW plant and other industries can feel the economic pulse throbbing.

This rapid growth has created big problems. For example, Spartanburg saw junkyards sprout in outlying neighborhoods, threatening property values and peace of mind. But unlike their Alabama counterparts, Spartanburg's leaders could take action. They passed an ordinance to control these nuisances. They had home rule backing them up.

But where is the leadership that would champion home rule in Alabama, giving urban counties the authority to manage their growth and address difficult problems? The leadership must begin with a governor and legislators who are willing to risk their political futures by doing what's right for local government, even if that means incurring the wrath of special interests. Alabama's citizens deserve to govern themselves locally just as people elsewhere enjoy that right.

In 1901, the state's constitutional convention was debating whether to hand legislators control over local government. Big landowners and their industrial allies wanted to concentrate power in Montgomery and restrict democracy. John A. Rogers, a delegate from Sumter County, rose to challenge these "Big Mules."

"I would like to know if there are men sitting here in this convention who think that their people have exhausted their senses in sending them here," he said. "Why is it that these people can select such fine representatives to the Legislature and yet it is feared that they won't be able to select satisfactory County Boards . . . ?"

The question rings true nearly a century later as we struggle to correct the error of that convention. Yet the recent example of South Carolina raises hope. If that state's citizens can overcome the lords of privilege and march forward under home rule, then so can Alabama's.

As Ray and Barbara Stevens might warn you from behind their shut windows, our collective failure to act invites the hogs to frolic.

RON CASEY

Our Rotten Constitution
Needs to Go

October 2, 1999, *Birmingham News*

The Alabama Constitution is an unworkable, insulting fraud. The only reason we haven't thrown this worthless piece of Byzantine baloney out the window is because a bunch of powerful interests use it to maintain ownership of our state government.

When I read Samford University president Thomas Corts's piece about reforming the constitution in our "Review & Comment" section a couple of weeks ago, I wanted to cheer.

He's absolutely right. The constitution doesn't make all of Alabama's problems. But it makes all of Alabama's problems worse.

Choose any issue you can think of—from cures for our franchise tax to Jefferson County's occupational tax woes, from budgeting to home rule—and they all are stuck in this gummed-up ball of Rube Goldberg legalisms we call a constitution.

Its obstruction is intentional, too. It is working as planned.

In 1875, Democrats recaptured Alabama's state House after Reconstruction. But many counties were still run by the "radical Republicans." So those in Montgomery drew up a constitution which said that before anything could take place at the county level, the state legislature had to approve.

Years later, when the current constitution was adopted in 1901, those same constrictions were left in place along with measures to keep property taxes abysmally low for the farm, timber, coal, and ore industries which ran the state. Then it was all hawked to the people in the name of "white supremacy" as a means to disfranchise black voters—in effect, beginning the atrocious collection of Jim Crow laws the state would ultimately be infected by.

There is more than one way to fix the constitution. You could reform it one article at a time, the way the Judicial Article was rewritten several years ago. You could better organize it and set up some general amendments that would cancel the need for so many specific amendments.

My choice would be to burn it, dance on the ashes, and start all over. For two reasons:

Most people don't understand how atrocious the origin of this thing is. It was not about disfranchising blacks; it was about disfranchising anyone who wasn't like the affluent white men who drew it up. Their discussion during the constitutional convention was centered on making a state to be run by the "virtuous and wise"—meaning themselves.

They had promised to let the people vote on the document they created, so they would need the votes of poor whites for passage. But they put in it so many insidious clauses that would prevent the sons and daughters of those same poor whites from voting in following years that by 1941, one study says, more whites were disfranchised than blacks.

In that year, 600,000 whites and 520,000 blacks were disfranchised. The state had only 440,000 registered voters.

Secondly, the people of Alabama never approved this constitution. It passed by massive voter fraud. According to the courageous historian Malcolm McMillan, who published his *Constitutional Development in Alabama* in 1955, the voting went this way:

In fifty-four Alabama counties it totaled 76,263 against to 72,389 for. But in twelve Black Belt counties (which had African American populations of more than two-thirds), the vote was a lopsided 36,224 to 5,471 in favor. Is it more reasonable to believe that blacks voluntarily voted to disfranchise themselves, or to believe that ballot boxes were stuffed like Christmas geese?

One argument against a new constitution is that it would create a lot of new lawsuits to test its subtleties. But when in our history have we not had a lot of new lawsuits? And it's not like we haven't done this before. This is our fifth state constitution, not our first.

A second argument is that the delegates elected to a constitutional convention might be the same folks who now run our state government. Thus, they would draw up a document for interest groups, instead of people. But surely more nonpolitical people would be interested in running as convention delegates, since this would not require a long commitment, like the legislature.

Can you imagine the people of Alabama, black and white, rich and poor, young and old, male and female, coming together to say to the world that we want a fresh start, one that repudiates the poisonous, racist document at the heart of our government?

We're bound to come up with a better constitution than the rotting carcass our state is ruled by now. It is impossible to do any worse.

BAILEY THOMSON

Looking for Cover

January 2, 2000, Birmingham News

Much of my education occurred on Saturday afternoons at the Palace Theater in Aliceville. Admission cost a child one dime, and the matinees typically featured westerns with cowboy stars such as Hopalong Cassidy and Audie Murphy.

The hero didn't look for trouble. But when some threat arose to a law-abiding community, he did the right thing, galvanizing citizens to resist the bad guys.

Often, just when the outlaws were about to win in a shoot-out, our hero would declare to his sidekicks, "I'm going on ahead. You cover me!"

Those lines signaled that the hero was about to stick his neck out and draw hostile fire. The audience learned an important lesson: leadership is about taking risks for great causes. It is also about motivating people to seek the common good.

Here in the last week of this tumultuous century, I wonder: where are the leaders in Alabama who might encourage our citizens to do what's right for themselves and their posterity? Our officials often say they are doing what people want them to do. But relatively few dare to get out front—ahead of the opinion polls and the old tired wisdom that says nothing changes in Alabama.

As I travel around our state, I hear a radically different version of the old cowboy line that used to thrill me at the Palace. Citizen activists say, "We can't expect our politicians to take the lead on this particular issue. So we have to give them cover."

In other words, citizens trying to address serious problems must go first and draw the fire before politicians will join the battle.

Certainly, some caution is understandable. Even a courageous politician can address only a few major issues at a time. But prudence too often becomes timidity. Many politicians are reluctant to challenge powerful interest groups and jeopardize their campaign contributions. As a consequence, we don't hear enough of them talk about tax reform, home rule, and other fundamental issues.

The public, meanwhile, has to be educated. This can be difficult during a campaign when political discourse often is squeezed into sound bites of less than a minute. Still, it doesn't take much longer than a minute to realize Alabama is in trouble—deep trouble. Our state has not done those things a well-constituted citizenry should do.

Consider our wretched tax system. We've had two blue-ribbon groups study it in the last decade. They've both concluded the system rewards the wealthy with low property and income taxes and punishes the poor with high sales taxes. Yet, our state staggers from one crisis to the next as our leaders try to patch a regressive system rather than reform it.

At the local level, meanwhile, officials lack the authority they need to address the runaway sprawl that afflicts our urban counties with traffic jams and environmental damage. Without home rule, local governments cannot manage growth properly.

So far, Gov. Don Siegelman has committed little of his popularity to addressing these big problems. Yet, he knows our neighbors have moved far ahead of us in many significant ways because their leaders have acted boldly.

For example, Georgia has a broader tax base that provides about $500 more per capita to invest in schools and other services. It's probably no coincidence that Georgia's economic growth rate consistently exceeds the national average, while Alabama's rate regularly falls below the U.S. benchmark.

North Carolina, meanwhile, has tied new school spending to high standards, and it rewards teachers for good performance. By contrast, many of Alabama's public schools look and smell like run-down tenements, while accountability depends upon a simplistic high-stakes test that is not based on our prescribed courses of study.

The biggest barrier to democracy in Alabama is the state's constitution, which has 661 amendments. In the dark recesses of its verbiage lie prohibitions and restrictions that prevent politics from working. Our constitution is not fundamental law in the proper sense; rather, it is special-interest legislation that shamelessly protects an unacceptable status quo. The result is that reformers cannot get at many of the major issues such as tax reform and home rule because they are bound in a legal knot.

The constitution has reflected bad faith toward government since the beginning. Its framers in 1901 sought to disfranchise black voters and many of the poor whites as well. The plot would not have succeeded under honest elections, but proponents won ratification by stuffing ballot boxes—a fraud well documented by our historians. We have lived with that immoral legacy ever since, even as the federal courts and Congress have freed us from some of the most blatant injustices.

To his credit, Secretary of State Jim Bennett recently championed a convention to draft a new state constitution. Another Republican, state representative Mac Gipson of Prattville, says he will ask the legislature to call such a convention.

So where are the other leaders who will step forward and slay this monstrosity? Where are the other leaders who will tell the truth—that we cannot fix our many problems in Alabama until we first create a sound blueprint for government?

I'm afraid that most of them are looking for cover.

If that is true, then we citizens must launch a reform movement ourselves. We begin with a determination to make something big happen. By that, I mean citizens can come together in civic, professional, and business organizations and demand a new constitution—one that will lay out in clear language a modern and equitable set of rules for our democracy.

A new constitution would establish a level playing field so our political parties could act upon their programs. In turn, we citizens could hold our elected leaders accountable for results, rather than accept their excuses for failure. In other words, we could push those important issues that are bound up in the present constitution down to where democracy can address them.

Bennett and Gipson have the right idea about a convention. This method would be harder for special interests to control, as opposed to having the legislature rewrite the constitution article by article. More important, a convention would invite more good people to get involved in civic affairs. We might see capable new leaders enter the arena.

Skeptics offer many reasons for why a constitutional movement cannot succeed. For example, the people who control much of this state's politics fear giving citizens real power. Yet I'm amused at how often these skeptics wish aloud we could really change things in Alabama.

Well, I think we can. As St. Paul advises, "Let us not be weary in well doing, for in due season we shall reap, if we do not give up."

Yes, it is tempting to walk away and disengage from problems that beset our state. But like many other citizens, I still believe in heroic action. I still believe we the people can challenge our circumstances and change them, if only we do not give up.

If this were a Saturday afternoon at the movies, we might hope some noble stranger would ride into town and rescue us, all in about the time it takes for a double feature to finish. But in this real world, we have to figure out how we can save ourselves—and save Alabama.

I'm willing to bet my picture show dime we can do it.

RON CASEY

The Cricket's Song

September 2, 1990, *Birmingham News,* from Pulitzer Prize–
winning "What They Won't Tell You about Your Taxes" series

In the sanctum of a summer night, the cricket sings an ageless benediction.

Those few still moments before bone weariness turns to sleep, how many gen-erations of Alabamians have heard its chorus behind a feeble resurrection of am-bition numbed by the fatigue of just getting by?

Exhaustion. Desperation. Ambivalence.

A dull-edged longing, too, subtle and relentless as the cricket's cry, that things might get better for their children and for their children's children.

They hear it in 1918, in the same year their legislature spends $135,000 on pre-vention of disease in farm animals, but only $26,000 on public health.

"And you will find her [Alabama] third in production of iron and ore; fourth in the production of pig iron; sixth in the production of coal; ninth in the pro-duction of cotton," says the Russell Sage Foundation of New York in a report to Gov. Charles Henderson.

"But when you come to the record of her social development you find Ala-bama second or third in the profit derived from the labor of her convicts, but far down in her efforts for their reformation; high in illiteracy, but low in pub-lic school education . . . high in the protection of health of hogs and cattle, but low in the protection of the health of people."

The report recommends tax reform.

The children of the parents of 1918 hear it in the 1930s, even as James Agee is in the midst of his self-centered account of life among his personal gallery of Alabama tenant farmers, *Let Us Now Praise Famous Men:* "They live in a steady shame and insult of discomforts, insecurities, and inferiorities, piecing these to-gether into whatever semblance of comfortable living they can, and the whole of it is a stark nakedness of makeshifts and the lack of means; yet they are also profoundly anesthetized . . . the deepest and most honest and incontrovertible rationalization of the middle-class Southerner is that they are 'used to it.'"

The words come just after Gov. B. M. Miller ends a long battle with the legislature, and voters, over how to bail out a state bankrupted by Depression.

The Brookings Institution's exhaustive study of Alabama government recommends radical tax reform.

Yet Miller has to try three times to enact even a limited income tax plan to keep the legislature from funding the whole burden of Depression debts from sales taxes on "the little man."

The children of the tenant farms are the workers of the factories by 1947. They hear the cricket's call in the beds of "company houses" as a soot-stained Birmingham writhes to maturity. A sparse metropolis it is.

"At war's end, the once Magic City relapsed again. Birmingham in 1947 had no local symphony orchestra, chamber music society, community theater, outstanding parks or downtown clubs," writes historian Virginia Van der Veer Hamilton.

"Even its zoo had closed. Schools and other public services were starved by a low property tax structure."

The legislature's Interim Committee on Revenue, composed largely of businessmen, publishes its report "The Alabama Revenue System" that same year.

It sharply criticizes the state's property taxes, saying smaller landowners are harder hit by them than large landholders. It charges the whole tax system banks heavily on the poor and "is not conducive to the economic development of the state."

It recommends tax reform.

The children of those children hear it in the 1960s and 1970s as farm and manufacturing jobs plummet, while racial turmoil is on the upswing.

A group of schoolchildren charges the property tax system robs them of decent support for an education. They and others go into federal court to do what the legislature had not done for decades—accomplish significant tax reform.

The court throws out the ridiculously low, out-of-balance assessments that shield big landholders from the property tax and orders a statewide reevaluation. But the legislature steps in with other shields.

In 1967, the percentage of property tax value subject to taxation is lowered from sixty percent to thirty percent. Later from thirty percent to fifteen percent. Later from fifteen percent to ten percent. Even from that level in 1982 passage of a "current use law" cuts the taxes paid on some of the state's largest tracts in half.

The last thing they (the legislature) won't tell you about your taxes this week is that for a hundred years, the state of Alabama has not been on your side.

Many lawmakers have been. Some governors have been. But the state itself, through its intricate webs of institutionalized favoritism and the inadequacies of its services, has not.

It acts through contrivance, to protect the sacred cows. It acts through convenience, to pass taxes that meet the least resistance instead of justice.

The result is a disgraceful system that pats the powerful on the back instead of lending a helping hand to the struggling.

We have the lowest property taxes in the nation. Yet we rank near the bottom in funding for our schools.

We are one of the poorest states in the union. Yet our tax system overburdens our poor.

We rust in the shadows of the Sun Belt. Yet our taxes and services cloud economic growth.

Alabama has a higher percentage of residents who are natives than almost any other state. We are the sons and daughters of slaves and planters, of tenant farmers and merchants.

We are a people who carved a world healing center out of a mountain of iron; who turned cotton fields into moon ship factories; who, even in the shackles of poverty and the disunity of prejudice, relentlessly crawled forward.

And we have done all that though our state has not been on our side.

Fifteen years from now, the cricket will pray an ageless benediction over the ambitions of our children.

II

Education and Children

Casey and Thomson wrote often about education. Both lamented what they saw as inadequate funding for public K–12 education, but also the impediment that the Alabama Education Association—the powerful teachers union led by Paul Hubbert—often represented to fundamental reform. Thomson also wrote penetratingly and presciently about the sprawl of higher education within the state, and how colleges protected themselves, though not students and taxpayers, by having legislators on the payroll.

Child welfare apart from education was a topic that consumed Casey, and he immersed himself in the details of both the local and state response to such issues as foster care, juvenile justice, and violence as it enveloped the low-income youth of Birmingham in the 1980s and '90s.

RON CASEY

Parched Earth

April 6, 1993, *Birmingham News,* from
"A Matter of Pride" series

Thunder rolls at the edge of the skyline.

Every other Southern state has pushed hard to better the poorest schools in the country. Some are on their second wave of reform. Alabama has come up dry.

Lightning flashes as one study after another warns of the devastation.

A fifth of Alabama's workplace is an endangered species, says one. Their low-pay, low-skill jobs may not survive. Better than half the state's adult population does not have a high school diploma, says another. Yet two out of three jobs that might have come here in the next decade will require college training.

Thunder and lightning.

No rain.

The air was fired with skepticism, not electricity, as Gov. Guy Hunt called together yet another study commission a year ago.

It was the third such panel in two years. The governor's other high-profile commissions spent months studying education's massive problems, with the anemic result being only passage of an improvement act with no money to make it work.

When the third reform panel was named, however, it became clear what was in mind. Members would represent the most powerful economic and education factions in the state. They were supposed to strike a deal that could elbow through our unruly legislature.

Their plan wasn't perfect. It wasn't even tied to the unfunded act. And it was massively complex, trying in one swoop to reform Alabama's unfair, archaic tax system and deal with most of the funding, teaching, and accountability problems in primary, secondary, and higher education.

It seemed possible, though. Publicly embraced by every major state official, two thousand citizens marched on their state capitol to support it.

Yet over the confusing, stultifying weeks in our legislature, it died from a thousand small wounds. What happened?

The question is crucial, especially now that Governor Hunt has decided not to appeal Judge Gene Reese's findings about the sorry state of our schools. The remedy ultimately must be fashioned in the same arena where reform was hacked apart last year. Unless we understand the forces against our children there, it will not be the one this state desperately needs.

The answer is that unlike in other eras, there is no overriding power structure in Alabama which can, for better or worse, wring order from anarchy. We are in a political dust devil.

Throughout most of this state's history, there have been two pillars of politics.

On one side were the ultra-conservative Bourbon Democrats, scions of timber, cotton, iron ore, and coal. They wanted a bare minimum of taxes and services.

They controlled Alabama by making it one of the most undemocratic states in the union. Their rule denied the vote to blacks and poor whites with poll taxes. It silenced the voices of thousands in government by refusing to draw fair legislative districts for six decades.

On the other side, the names changed, but the idea of making government work harder for common people was always present. They were the populists, the progressives, the Folsomites.

After World War II, one blow after another hit both those columns like wrecking balls.

The rule of steel and cotton collapsed. In the 1960s alone, Alabama lost more than half its farm jobs as sharecropping died. Birmingham's steel mills hired thirty thousand in the 1930s, but would have jobs for less than a tenth of that a few decades later, as computerization and foreign competition took their toll.

At the same time, the civil rights movement sent shock waves through sixty years of saturating, rigidly enforced custom.

Court decisions struck down the barriers to government of the people. Yet the revolutionary changes also demolished a segregated economic system which, in a state ever scarred by scarcity, placed poor whites a step ahead of blacks.

In the wake of the chaos emerged George C. Wallace. With a blatant play to hubris, fear, and prejudice, Wallace crushed the pillars of Alabama politics. Neither side could stand up to him. Neither wanted to try.

National movements brought a new wind. Trial lawyers organized to improve state court systems. As they beefed up lobbying in the Alabama legislature, another key player noticed.

"When Paul Hubbert was elected president of the Alabama Education Association," says one historian, "he had enough sense to understand what Wallace had done to the political framework, and to understand what the trial lawyers were doing."

AEA merged with a large number of black teachers in a separate group headed by Joe Reed. Then it was molded into a major political force.

The dust whipped up. When business saw what AEA and the trial lawyers were doing, it kicked up its lobbying. Then labor felt it had to do the same. On and on it ratcheted upward, until by 1992 a legislature which in the 1950s had less than a dozen lobbyists, was facing four hundred.

Into that den marched the reformers last year.

Into a den in which the mold of government no longer fits the state. So many of our tax laws were locked into Alabama's constitution to preserve the advantages of economic forces whose power was waning. To change them, you need a three-fifths majority in the legislature and a statewide vote of the people.

Into a den in which lawmakers have been apprenticed for 150 years to distrust schools. The argument over more money or more accountability didn't begin with Governor Hunt. It began in the 1830s, when Alabama schools lost most of their reserves because, lacking support from the legislature, they tried to grow more money by investing in a state bank which ultimately failed.

The argument resurfaces again and again throughout our history. Lawmakers lacking revenues skimp on funding. When education is shabby, they blame waste.

Thunder and lightning.

No rain.

BAILEY THOMSON

Suffer the Little Ones

October 13, 1998, *Mobile Press-Register,*
from "Dixie's Broken Heart" series

Two governors—old South and new.

In Alabama, Gov. Fob James squirmed, dodged, and lied to avoid higher tobacco taxes. Result? Lightly taxed companies aren't accountable for the horrific
cost their tobacco inflicts on Alabama citizens.

But Florida, under Gov. Lawton Chiles, has forced Big Tobacco to pay res-
titution. What's more, Florida is investing that money in the next generation,
rescuing children not only from smoking but also from poor health, abuse, and
neglect. The payoff will be healthy, productive workers who'll keep Florida competitive for good jobs.

A similar vision drives a coalition for children in Alabama, whose members
include judges, district attorneys, legislators, civic leaders, and other concerned
people. They want to spend $85 million a year on a group of programs known
as Children First. Alabama would secure the money by either assessing or taxing
tobacco companies. In turn, this investment would generate another $45 million
in federal matching dollars.

Last spring, the coalition sensed victory, but Big Tobacco's hired guns am-
bushed supporters in the House Rules Committee. The lobbyists' maneuver de-
layed action long enough for their flunkies to strip away the tobacco tax. The legislature went on to approve the programs, but it provided no immediate money
to pay for them.

Governor James was in the thick of the dirty work. "He's run the dagger in
our back every chance he's gotten," lamented a veteran of this fight. The governor's disgraceful behavior occurred after he promised Attorney General Bill
Pryor and others that he would support the tobacco tax for Children First.

Mr. Pryor and a bipartisan coalition managed to salvage a promise from the legislature that the children's programs would receive the first $85 million a year from Alabama's share of any national settlement with tobacco companies. The settlement is no certainty, of course. Big Tobacco recently foiled Congress's attempt to levy more taxes.

Meanwhile, Governor James was soon talking about diverting any potential settlement share to pay for college scholarships. This treachery came from a man who had the gall to declare 1997 as the "Year of the Child."

With a national tobacco settlement still uncertain, voters can consider what Governor James's perfidy so far has denied Alabama's children, a fourth of whom live in poverty:

More than 100,000 children won't get health insurance, because their families can't pay for it without state help.

Thousands of children will languish on long waiting lists for subsidized child care.

Growing numbers of juveniles in trouble won't receive adequate treatment and supervision.

The consequences of such inaction will cost many times more than what Children First proposes to spend on prevention. For example, advocates for these programs argue that every dollar spent immunizing children against diseases such as measles saves more than $10 in treatment costs later.

With the failure to pay Children First, Alabama perpetuated its worst old ways. Big interests, such as tobacco companies, prevail in Montgomery, while the poor and the weak suffer. No wonder that a national comparison ranks Alabama at the bottom in efforts to help children from poor families.

Now, let's consider what's happening elsewhere—and what visionary leadership can do for a state.

Governor Chiles is Florida's best granddaddy. After retiring from the U.S. Senate, he ran for governor in 1990, vowing to help Florida's mothers and children. He refused to take the special interests' money, limiting campaign contributions to just $100. That independence showed in 1997, when he wrested from the tobacco companies an $11.3 billion settlement for Florida—money the legislature is now investing in kids.

At the end of his second term, Governor Chiles looks upon a remarkably better state for its youngest citizens. Much of the improvement owes to his tenacity as their greatest champion. Contrast some of Florida's legislative action in 1998 with Alabama's shameful surrender to Big Tobacco:

By combining federal and state dollars, Florida will provide health insurance to an additional 254,000 children.

The state will hire about two hundred new investigators to fight child abuse.

Another 23,900 kids will get quality child care—a lifesaver for working parents who can't afford to pay the full cost.

Such victories crown this governor's leadership with a lasting legacy, as healthy and educated kids grow up to be successful parents themselves. Indeed, more of them are alive today because Governor Chiles fought to reduce infant deaths.

Under a program Governor Chiles sponsored called Healthy Start, women receive nursing care for themselves and their infants, breast-feeding instruction, parenting classes, and other help through a network of community agencies. More than a million mothers and infants have received help, and Florida's mortality rate has dropped sixteen percent since 1992 to beat the national average.

Like Governor James in Alabama, Governor Chiles used his 1997 legislative address to extol children—but the Florida leader's words meant something. He educated his listeners about how the first three years of life can set a child's future, good or bad. This time is critical, he said, because new research shows how fast a newborn's brain develops.

At birth, the brain has about 100 billion neurons. By age one that figure explodes to 1,000 trillion. Talking to children, showing them games, even playing classical music to them during these first years can make a difference of twenty IQ points—an astounding implication for the state as it struggles to provide good child care for mothers who are leaving welfare for work.

How ironic that much of the research Governor Chiles cited was conducted at the University of Alabama at Birmingham, under the guidance of child-development experts Craig and Sharon Ramey. Their acclaimed work over the past thirty years demonstrates how high-quality health care and child care pay extraordinary dividends in stimulating toddlers' brain development. With sufficient intervention, even children who have a high risk of failure can enter school and keep up with their more fortunate peers.

Without extra help, Craig Ramey warns, such children often never catch up, and schools tag them as slow learners. "We can't expect special ed to reverse a lifetime of inadequate experiences. It can't make up for what the children have missed," he says.

Governor Chiles grasped this great insight from specific research and saw the potential to break the cycle of poverty and neglect that has bedeviled our region. "Education must start at gestation," he told Florida's legislators.

If only Alabama had such leadership and common sense in its governor's chair. Or if only there were more legislators willing to pull the voting lever for what's right, rather than jerk at the ends of the lobbyists' strings.

RON CASEY

Poor Kids, Poor Scores

December 22, 1996, *Birmingham News,* unsigned editorial

School systems with higher test scores in Alabama usually have fewer children in poverty or in single-parent families.

You can prove that with a computer, as staff writer Chris Roberts did this week, comparing population information to school rankings.

Or you can do it with common sense.

In even the best of single-parent households, the lone parent doesn't have as much time to spend on school preparation.

And upper-income homes usually are upper-income because they are well educated. There is a direct correlation between education and earning power. People who have a good education and know its worth are more likely to push their own children in school.

What is shocking, however, is that while we have a much larger number of at-risk children than most states, we have done a lousy job of trying to help them.

It is a devastating shortcoming economically, and a shameful commentary on our attitude about the less fortunate.

A quarter of Alabama's school-age children lived in poverty in the 1990 census, and forty-six percent met the criteria for reduced-price lunches.

But, according to the Southern Regional Education Board, we have been the only state in the region without any state program to provide them special help.

An informal survey done by Jim Williams at the Public Affairs Research Council of Alabama shows that when you compare Alabama to a few other states that use standardized tests to measure school achievement (Utah, Washington, Virginia, and Georgia) there is a consistent finding:

The schools in Alabama with small numbers of at-risk students (like the Mountain Brooks and the Hoovers) do better than similar schools in those states. The schools here with a large number of at-risk kids do substantially worse.

We have not had programs like the one begun in Georgia in 1991 which will soon put $185 million a year into preparing four-year-olds for kindergarten. Or the Reading Recovery Program set up in Arkansas in 1988, where one-on-one tutoring makes sure first-graders get a sound start.

In fact, it was only in the last legislative session that at-risk programs got any money from the state. Pushed by state superintendent Ed Richardson, lawmakers came up with $28 million to help, while school districts are all being asked to develop local plans for how to aid needy children in their areas.

Many of those districts will call that money a godsend, and it is. But it is also a day late and a dollar short compared to what other states have been doing. At $100 a head, it is ten times less than what has been called for in a school funding lawsuit court order.

The next legislature needs to make absolutely certain that money not only continues to flow but is increased.

Obviously the best way to prepare a child for school is concerned parents. That's not even at question.

The problem lies in how Alabama's society responds if that child isn't ready. Do we help, or do we stand by and allow him or her to founder in school and become an underproductive worker or, worse, a ward of the state?

For too long, Alabama's answer has been the latter. You don't need a computer to tell you that's not only callous but stupid.

BAILEY THOMSON

Faces from the Future

October 18, 2000, *Mobile Press-Register,*
from "Century of Shame" series

Even before classes began this fall, Principal Pam Adams was greeting new families at Castlen Elementary School. They had moved to Grand Bay, where subdivisions are muscling out cotton in the lush, flat land of southern Mobile County.

Castlen opened in 1968 to serve 350 children. Today, it has three times that number. The school has the same kitchen and cafeteria it had thirty-two years ago, the small size of which requires the first lunch shift to begin at 10 a.m.

Ms. Adams has to pack many of the newcomers into twenty-seven portable classrooms. Children in those cramped quarters lose as much as an hour every day trooping back and forth to lunch or the library, or lining up at two portable restrooms. Ms. Adams keeps a daily vigil for any suspicious odors rising from the little sewage treatment plant behind the school, hoping it can handle the demand.

Recently, she learned the local water board expects one thousand families to move into the area each year for at least the next five years.

"It's a great community," says Ms. Adams, who is in her third year at Castlen. Parents recently raised $10,000 selling candy to buy six new computers and a dozen printers.

Still, on August 17, 1999, local voters helped defeat a Mobile County property tax increase that would have generated $22 million a year to build new schools and renovate old ones like Castlen. Then came another blow: local legislators refused to approve a less-costly alternative that would have at least provided relief for Castlen's crowding.

In both instances, Mobile County's schoolchildren lost out because a rattletrap state constitution fails to move education into Alabama's new Mercedes age. That document belongs in the nineteenth century, when mule-drawn wagons hauled cotton to the gins. It's obsolete today, when information floods the Internet and learning is a life-long endeavor.

The 1901 constitution prevents local government from levying reasonable property taxes to support public schools. Thus, local officials must beg the legislature to amend the constitution's stingy limits.

This procedure gives legislators a blank check to meddle back home. They can add whatever conditions they please to an amendment or tax act before sending it to local voters for approval.

Worse, the constitution turns legislators into petty tyrants because it doesn't allow county governments to pass local ordinances. The legislature writes the local laws instead. In practice, such lawmaking is done by the legislators who represent the county. Under a rule known as "local courtesy," however, a single state senator among that small delegation can veto any proposal—no matter how desperately folks back home need relief.

These provisions helped a group of landowners and other opponents defeat the proposed school tax increase in Mobile County last year. First, they turned to their friends in the local legislative delegation, especially Sen. George Callahan. These legislators cut the school board's request by a third before agreeing to let local voters decide the fate of the tax. Next, they backed up the voting date to a time when schools would be closed and many parents on vacation.

It was an easy victory for opponents, who kept harping on distrust of the school system—while doing all they could to foster such attitudes.

Last April, the Mobile County Commission came forward with a bold plan to pump $75 million into the school system as a down payment on $250 million in construction needs. Commission president Sam Jones received a thunderous standing ovation from business and civic leaders when he proposed diverting several county revenue sources to support this bond issue.

But Mr. Callahan, a Republican still nursing political wounds from old battles with the commission's two Democrats, was lying in wait. He pushed an alternative that would siphon to schools a portion of the revenues from the county's one-cent sales tax, crippling other services. There was no way the county commissioners could buy his scheme.

A furious Sen. Vivian Figures of the Mobile County delegation blasted Mr. Callahan's tactics. In the uproar, the commission's plan died in the committee room, along with hopes for relieving crowding in Mobile County schools.

This fall, when the doors opened to a new year, school superintendent Harold Dodge informed employees that the system was having to cut its budget by several million dollars. Already, it had reduced spending on textbooks, eliminated a homework hotline, and hired fewer teachers than the schools needed.

It's understandable that many frustrated school advocates in Alabama are ready to give up the fight for more property taxes, although this traditional source continues to sustain schools around the country.

The sales tax might seem to be an attractive option for schools because, unlike property and income taxes, it is not restricted by Alabama's 1901 constitution. And the Mobile County Commission already has authority to levy another penny. But such a move would be unwise for two reasons:

- First, adding a penny would increase the tax burden on poor people because they pay the same sales-tax rates as everyone else. Indeed, they pay an even higher percentage of their incomes for necessities such as groceries, which means that sales taxes hit them harder.

    Mississippi and some other states offset such unfairness by giving poor citizens a break on income taxes. Alabama largely ignores its poor. Our state constitution requires a family of four to begin paying taxes on its income at just $4,600, the lowest threshold in the nation.

    The rich are treated preferentially, of course. The top tax rate—five percent—applies to poor and rich alike. And Alabama is one of only three states that allow a full deduction for federal income taxes. Because people in the top brackets pay higher federal taxes, this benefit provides minimal relief for most Alabama families.
- Second, adding another penny would make local public services even more dependent on a regressive and fickle tax source. Already, consumers in the city of Mobile pay nine cents in sales taxes on every $1 of purchases. Push the rate higher and watch more business flee to the lower rates of unincorporated areas.

    At present, the city derives about $524 per capita—fifty-six percent of its total revenues—from its four-cent share of sales taxes. By contrast, the city gets just $41 per capita from property taxes.

What we have in Alabama, then, is the worst tax system that our unfair, antiquated constitution can inspire. That system also is one of the least adequate in providing services that Alabamians need. Certainly, it treats public schools like orphans.

Alabama places dead last among states in local support for schools. It is hardly surprising that Alabama also is near the bottom in per-student spending.

Such rankings can be heart-wrenching when you put a child's face on them. That's not hard to do, either. In fact, there are 65,000 faces—all belonging to

Mobile County's students. They're looking out the windows at us from one hundred schools, where buildings often sag from age, or from 520 portable classrooms.

The young minds deserve better than what politics has served up for them. They are, after all, the faces of the future—even as their state constitution looks resolutely toward the past.

RON CASEY

Lottery Fails Fairness, Priority Tests

August 20, 1999, *Birmingham News*

There's an old story about a man desperately looking for his car keys under a street lamp. A friend says he wants to help and asks where the keys were last seen.

"Over there," says the man, pointing to a spot one hundred yards away. "So why are you looking for them under this lamp?" the friend asks.

"Well," says the man, "the light's better here."

That pretty much sums up the way I feel about a state lottery.

It would be different and refreshing if we could get through this lottery debate without demonizing one another.

Don Siegelman is not the devil incarnate for proposing one. He's a pragmatic politician who genuinely cares about children. He sees a lot of needs in education and polls showing that a lottery may be the most likely place to get more revenue. This is a practical, but not perfect, move I would give him credit for thinking of—one that might kick-start education.

On the other hand, people who object to the lottery for moral reasons are not all holier-than-thous. The state won't simply allow someone to play the lottery; it will advertise to entice people to play. Having the state sucker citizens into losing their money bothers me, too.

But let's think for a moment only about the bottom line here: Is the state raising money in the fairest way? Is it using the money raised on the top priority?

The answer to both is no. This has more to do with what's popular than with what is right.

In 1996, Citizens for Tax Justice named Alabama one of its "terrible ten" states—those whose tax systems bank most heavily on the poor and middle class rather than the affluent.

The poorest twenty percent of taxpayers in this state pay 11.6 percent of their incomes to taxes. The middle class pays 9 percent. The top level pays 4.8 percent.

Instead of doing things (like taking the sales tax off food) to improve that sorry picture, we're working on a lottery which will make it worse. Everybody plays the lottery when there is a big pot. But week in and week out, the regular customers are the poor.

And state representative John Rogers is right: the way things are set up now, the poor will likely see the least benefit from this program. That's because the state will deduct any money students get from Pell Grants or other federal aid to the poor from their state scholarships.

The poor shoulder the heaviest burden in. The poor get less out. This is not something I think we should be proud of.

All the things Siegelman's lottery will buy are worthwhile—preschool programs to help kids get off to a good start, new technology for schools, and college tuition for any child who keeps good grades.

Put this in perspective, however. He projects the lottery will raise about $150 million a year. That breaks down to about $85 million for the scholarship program, $54 million for preschool, and $10 million for technology.

The lottery provides, then, $64 million for K–12 and $85 million for higher education.

But K–12 is the biggest problem in Alabama. Our schools spent $4,311 per student in 1996. That's $1,345 less per child than an average school system in the United States. We don't spend enough to let all our children compete in a world where well-trained minds mean more than strong backs.

Siegelman's $64 million is a tiny drop in a large bucket. Only a few years ago, the price tag for making our schools adequate was estimated at between $500 million to $1 billion more a year.

State superintendent Ed Richardson has been working on his own plan for adequacy which may be forthcoming shortly. Gaining support for the serious increases in funding it will take for that is a long shot, anyway. With Alabama's mossback timber and farm lobby having the smidgen of new money generated by a lottery to point to, I'd bet a jackpot against its chances.

In other states, like Georgia, such scholarship programs are icing on the cake. Here, we haven't baked the cake yet.

Siegelman's plan produces an emotional tug on folks worrying about how they're ever going to pay their children's college bill. (I feel it, too, with my own high school sophomore and seventh-grader.)

Too, a lottery offers the (false) promise that we can get something for nothing.

But, emotions aside, you can't vote for this as a matter of fairness or priority. The major thing going for it is that it's the only education improvement plan on the table.

It's the only plan, though, because—well, the light's better here.

BAILEY THOMSON

The Siren Song
of College Football

November 26, 1995, *Mobile Press-Register,*
from a series on higher education

The day before Auburn and Alabama marched their gladiators into the Iron Bowl's roaring arena, 660 Vanity Fair workers in Monroeville lost their jobs. A fourth of the apparel company's local payroll vanished before kickoff.

What does this tragedy have to do with higher education or, more to the point, with a gridiron rivalry of unequaled intensity?

Simply this: As Alabamians have cheered their teams and put football second only to God, the world has moved beyond us. We still revel in high national rankings, attested by the thousands of team banners fluttering atop car antennas. Yet our people face a more complex economic future, which will demand skills heretofore unimaginable. Reality stares out from the eyes of workers who won't be employed this Christmas season.

Just this year, 5,700 apparel jobs have evaporated—ten percent of Alabama's total. Town after town has watched companies cut back or flee.

Oh, it's nobody's fault, managers insist. They blame "market conditions." Translated, that means workers elsewhere will do those jobs more cheaply or efficiently. As America's companies have learned to compete globally, they have ruthlessly slashed their payrolls, often jettisoning low-skilled employees, which Alabama offers in abundance.

Indeed, a fourth of the state's workers lack high school diplomas. But even graduation doesn't guarantee mastery of basic skills. Forty percent of the state's college freshmen require catch-up courses in reading, writing, and math. Unless this sorry educational record improves, many more workers will have difficulty making payments on their pickups and refrigerators.

An odd feature of Alabama's educational system is how we starve the lower grades, while squandering taxpayers' generosity to higher education. Again, national rankings tell a story. But unlike football, it's not one that people like to hear.

Our state ranks at the bottom in per-capita spending on grades K–12. It shows. Little children attend crowded schools with leaking roofs because local taxpayers are too stingy to fix them. Few districts exceed national averages on standardized tests; most fall below the mark.

By contrast, Alabama luxuriates in taxpayer spending on colleges, ranking sixteenth nationally per capita. And no wonder. Since George Wallace began a building binge in the 1960s, politicians have scattered campuses like sugar plums around the state.

It's hardly surprising that many of these same politicians have grabbed a share of the loot. Some, including Mr. Wallace, shamelessly put themselves or their family members on the higher-ed payrolls. The legislature encourages this attitude: nineteen of its members work for the colleges, two of them as presidents.

In the South, only North Carolina taxes its citizens more heavily than Alabama for higher education. The former, however, has learned to curb its campuses' ambitions through statewide governance, while insisting upon high standards. As a result, the state's education dollars buy more. Meanwhile, North Carolina is a regional leader in both per-capita income and percentage of college graduates.

What a difference in Alabama, where more means less. With forty-seven public colleges, wasteful duplication saps quality, spreading those generous dollars too thinly. Many colleges fight rational governance and won't hold themselves accountable, even refusing to track how many graduates get jobs.

In Alabama, we have created a system we can no longer afford, one that soaks up nearly $1 billion in tax dollars a year, while giving too few assurances that academic programs match the state's needs.

Over the next few days, editorials in this space will explore the paradox of educational poverty among plenty. They will look at why Alabama gets a relatively small return on a large higher-ed investment. The situation is hardly hopeless, however. Strong leadership can bring this wayward system under control, as the conclusion will demonstrate.

It's not that Alabamians have to renounce their beloved football to have strong colleges. Gov. Fob James, who has promised to reform this system, was himself a fine Auburn tailback, who ran best in the mud, according to his coach, Shug Jordan. The problem is that we can't ignore what's happening off the field. People's lives depend on whether we put academic quality on at least a par with athletic achievement.

Right now, a cold winter awaits many Alabamians, whose prospects look bleak, while the stock market soars on the strength of America's reinvigorated companies. There is no quick political fix for our people's plight. But there is a long-term remedy. It lies in improving their skills and raising their educational levels. Never has higher education been more important.

BAILEY THOMSON

Thank God for Mississippi

October 15, 1998, *Mobile Press-Register,*
from "Dixie's Broken Heart" series

Inmates in Alabama's crowded prisons read, on average, at a level below the sixth grade. Most lack even basic job skills and work habits, which may explain, though not excuse, why they sell drugs, break in houses, and stick up convenience stores.

So it's a good thing to offer them education in hopes they'll learn to make an honest living. No fancy academic courses, mind you, but just basic instruction so inmates can earn the equivalent of a high school diploma or pick up rudimentary skills. Any good high school vocational or GED program could fit the bill nicely for a modest cost per inmate.

Only, Alabama doesn't do education so rationally—at least not when its voracious community colleges smell some action. They've grabbed the prison market for themselves—all $14 million worth. Moreover, the colleges are maneuvering to take over the state's entire adult education program, which is set to receive a big infusion of federal dollars.

Regarding the prisons, taxpayers might ask a simple question: What's the sense in having the community colleges, whose faculty earn the South's highest salaries for vocational teaching, instruct inmates who can barely read and write? Wouldn't it be more efficient to hire high school teachers to help prisoners earn their GEDs or learn basic job skills?

Good common sense, unfortunately, is scarce in Alabama. Its overbuilt two-year system is devoted more to achieving the ambitions of its college presidents and maintaining its well-padded payrolls than delivering the most efficient service to Alabama's citizens.

Indeed, all that stands in the way of even more grandiose expansion is the crippled Alabama Commission on Higher Education, which former governor

Albert Brewer established in 1969 to be a kind of policeman for higher ed. But ACHE recently saw angry legislators cut its budget $300,000 after the agency pointed out where Alabama could save and re-invest $100 million in college spending. Among the potential targets was prison education.

Even now, the colleges are fighting ACHE's legitimate authority to approve new programs and campuses. For example, Bevill State got a $500,000 appropriation to take over the former Walker College campus in Jasper, although ACHE has yet to pass judgment on the deal. Such arrogance on the colleges' part helps explain why Alabama has 182 college teaching sites, many of them unable to attract enough students to justify their existence.

The legislature is reluctant to rein in this wasteful expansion because the colleges pack such political clout. Consider, for example, that the next speaker of the House will probably be Rep. Seth Hammett, president of Lurleen B. Wallace State Junior College in Andalusia. Another president, Yvonne Kennedy of Mobile's Bishop State, will probably chair a powerful committee. Meanwhile, ten other legislators who work for the community colleges joined these two in the last legislature.

The state Board of Education has nominal authority over the two-year system. The board also oversees the state's public elementary and high schools. In plain truth, it's too big a job for an elected body—especially when these mostly amateur politicians go up against the heavy pros among the college presidents. It's hardly a secret that about a half dozen of the presidents, led by the wily former legislator Roy Johnson at Southern Union, run the show.

In fact, Alabamians might be surprised to know that their elected watchdog board lacks authority to initiate policy. That role belongs to the two-year college system's chancellor, Fred Gainous.

What's so heartbreaking about Alabama's predicament is that community colleges belong in the forefront of delivering efficient training to citizens. If managed properly, they can be a cost-saving way to meet future demands for higher education, while serving equally well as one-stop job centers for industries eager to hire skilled workers.

Alabama can find a model for reforming its two-year system by looking just over the state line into Mississippi. Our neighbor has developed a more rational way to govern its community colleges, while assigning them an even bigger role for the future.

Mississippi has the nation's oldest system of community colleges, which grew out of agricultural high schools in the 1920s. That long experience has taught people to cherish these institutions, but also to keep them current and responsive to new needs.

In 1986, the legislature created a separate governing agency for the colleges, removing their jurisdiction from the state education board. The reform freed the school board to concentrate on improving elementary and secondary education, while it focused attention on the special role of the two-year colleges in the state's development.

Meanwhile, the colleges kept their individual boards of trustees, which continue to oversee their day-to-day affairs and even hire their presidents. This local control combines with another admirable feature of Mississippi's system: local tax support. Each college serves a district that, in turn, levies a special property tax to help pay the costs. At present, Mississippi's colleges draw about eleven percent of their money from these local taxpayers.

The effect is to curb the kind of expensive adventurism that has led Alabama's system to expand into virtually every crossroads and branch head in the state. Unlike Mississippi's model, the local beneficiaries typically don't put up any dollars themselves to support these expansive sites, which fall like manna from a generous legislature. Thus, the game in Montgomery becomes one of bringing home the pork and often putting the local legislator on the college payroll.

Mississippi has another great feature: a strong conflict-of-interest law. It would be unthinkable, even illegal, for one of its college presidents to serve in the legislature. The same goes for its professors.

It's not that the administrators and teachers lack a voice. To the contrary, the colleges are a powerful and united force in Mississippi politics. The difference from Alabama's system, however, is that the educators deliberate as a group and decide among themselves what should be the system's priorities. Then they take that program to the legislature as a group, avoiding any freelance lobbying by individual schools.

What a difference from Alabama's dog-eat-dog methods, in which the politically strong presidents lobby legislators directly. This survival of the fittest approach has created what amounts to a two-tiered system—one in which the politically strong prosper at the expense of the weak.

Mississippi also has used its fifteen community colleges to create one-stop career centers, which train employees in partnership with local industries. The results have impressed outsiders as well, who see these centers as an ideal way to connect job-seekers to training and employers.

It's not that Alabama does a bad job of training people. In fact, many in Mississippi admire the versatility of Alabama's industrial job-training program, which operates as a separate wing under the chancellor's office. But Alabama's two-year system remains more concerned about pumping up enrollments and keeping jobs secure for tenured teachers than in emphasizing measurable performance. Thus, the heavy emphasis on courses such as cosmetology, which boost student counts but do little to make Alabama's economy more competitive.

Alabama's two-year colleges sprouted almost overnight, in contrast to the Mississippi system's evolutionary growth. The schools became prime pork for the late Gov. George Wallace's populist politics. Just look at the names of the thirty-odd colleges. Four of them have Wallace attached to them. Across this vast system, one can see the names of other politicians plastered on buildings as silent tributes to their favors.

But just as the Wallace era now stands out forlornly for the many lost opportunities to move Alabama forward with its neighboring states, so does the existing two-year system remind us of our political failure to harness the colleges to a rational development plan. Too often, they remain the petty dukedoms of their powerful presidents, rather than a united force for progress. And at their worst, the colleges confuse their mission with an insatiable lust for warm bodies—even those wearing prison white.

It's a legacy of power, greed, and growth for its own sake that Alabama can afford no more. Thank God for Mississippi for showing us a better way.

RON CASEY

Mother of Slain Boy
Deserves Explanation

June 30, 1995, *Birmingham News*

I have an invitation for the eight members of the House Rules Committee who voted down a plan to help fight juvenile violence last week.

Take a ride out to Central Park, as I did the same day of their vote. Off the Bessemer Superhighway, down through a relatively poor, but well-kept, neighborhood to a house with white paint and red trim. There they can explain their vote to Valerie White.

They should be prepared to make a very good case, however. Ms. White's fourteen-year-old son was gunned down in a drive-by shooting a year ago.

Michael Wilson was one of 176 homicides in Jefferson County in 1994. I remember the case, however, for a lot of reasons.

First, because my own son is fast approaching Michael's age. I have no idea how I would ever cope if he walked out the door and I never got to talk to him again.

Second, Michael was a special kid. He had never been in trouble. Shortly before his death, he won a trophy as the best algebra student at Jones Valley Middle School. After he died, his church renamed their teen retreat in his honor.

"He was a very mannerable young man, like the old students years ago who respected adults," one of his teachers said shortly after the shooting. "His mother was very education-oriented . . . They were a very different kind of inner-city family than what you normally see from this area."

Inside the living room of the house with the red trim, trophies won by Michael, his brother, Cedric, and his sister, Tomika, fill the shelves on either side of the fireplace. A family portrait sits on the coffee table. The house is clean. It has no air-conditioning.

Ms. White, a short, stout woman, talks about the last time she saw Michael alive.

They lived in an apartment on Tuscaloosa Avenue then. "Michael was eating pizza. He looked over at me with that grin he used to get and asked if he could please have the last piece."

After that, he and Cedric asked if they could go out on the porch of the apartment to play. While they were there, a red Blazer came by, someone shouted, "There he is," and a boy down the block held up his hands as though to surrender. A shooter fired, but he hit Michael instead.

Her story comes out mostly in resigned, matter-of-fact tones. But some parts are restrained bitterness: About how it took thirty minutes for police and an ambulance to come, because they said there was an address problem. About how the police wrestled Cedric away, thinking at first that he might be the shooter. About how, as Michael lay on the ground and his sister kept screaming and screaming, one officer walked over to her and said, "You might as well shut up, girl. Your brother's going to die, anyway."

The family moved away from Tuscaloosa Avenue, she says, because they just couldn't stand to be there anymore. But it didn't make the pain go away.

"People act like I ought to be over this. They say it's been a year," she says, wearing a small lapel button with Michael's picture on it. "But how can I get over this?"

Tomika has had a lot of emotional problems, Ms. White says. Cedric gets teased at West End High School. They call him a "punk" and "weak" for not getting a gun and going after whoever killed his brother. Ms. White tenses up anytime either of her other two children leave the house.

Part of the problem with "getting over it" is that no one has ever been convicted of Michael's death. Another boy, Keith Williams, originally told officers he could identify the trigger man, but changed his testimony in court. Then Williams himself was shot and critically wounded two days after his court appearance about two blocks away from where Michael had been killed.

Ms. White, a single mother who works at a kindergarten, has put up $1,000 of the family's money as a reward for anyone who has information about Michael's death. The state has offered no reward.

She doesn't want the killer to get the death penalty. "'Vengeance is mine,' the Lord said." But she does want him locked up. And she wants something else, too.

To have the feeling that someone really cares. She wanted to talk to the mayor and to the police chief, but neither returned her call, she says. People are working on the case, but many of them seem to be only doing a job. "Does anybody really care that my boy is dead?"

She would like simply for people to put a small blue ribbon on their door

July 22, the anniversary of Michael's death, just to say they have sympathy for him and for kids like him. In the meantime, she says she comforts herself with one thought. "Michael died like Jesus. He died for somebody else's sins. He gave that other boy a chance for salvation if he straightens himself out."

So I'd like for the honorables on the Rules Committee who voted down a cigarette tax that might really have helped stem juvenile crime and juvenile violence in Alabama to go out to Ms. White's house and tell her why they did that.

They can talk about how they had to because passing that tax might embarrass a Republican governor who pledged "no new taxes." About how those tobacco lobbyists, who led many of them into the room with their arms around their shoulders as they whispered in their ear, made good sense.

Maybe they can convince her they did the right thing. But I don't think so.

RON CASEY

A City in Denial

December 17, 1995, *Birmingham News,*
from "Children in the Storm" series

It easily could be a circle of hate, the group of adults and children around the fold-up tables in the meeting room of Shades Valley Presbyterian Church. But Carmen McCain, founder of Mothers against Violence, whose son died when a drive-by shooter randomly fired into a crowd, won't let it be.

Once a month they meet to sing hymns of love for God; to watch small children do dances of hope. Only near the end, when the parents gather on either side of a small podium, many carrying pictures of the children who are no more, does the sum of suffering in that room begin to well up in your eyes.

My daughter, Luanda, and I moved here five years ago, says Cynthia Johnson. She was twenty-one and wanted to be a nurse, I think, because I have multiple sclerosis. She went to school one night and I never saw her again. When they found her, she had been stabbed through the heart. They put her between a mattress and a box springs and set it on fire with gasoline. It took them a week to identify her body.

She leaves the podium. Another takes her place.

Nothing is worse than standing in a hospital and seeing your son with all those tubes in him, knowing he is dying, says Shirley Corley. My boy, Anthony, was eighteen. The ones who shot him made him get down on the ground. He told them he only had $6 and to please not kill him. But they shot him three times. I'm a nurse. I ought to be used to it. But at night, when I lie down to go to sleep, in my head I still see my son and those tubes.

We are in denial in Birmingham. The tragic parade of parents whose hearts will never heal goes on out of sight, out of mind for most of us. We see TV images of high school football players rolling across the field to avoid gang gunfire, and there is outrage; there are demands that something be done. But what must be done costs money; even more, it costs a continuing commitment to restore order in pockets where the ravages of poverty and the fall of social order have taken their toll.

When poverty was spread throughout the community, we had pity and support for "the poor." For the "inner-city poor" we have visions of gangs and guns—and fear.

My son, Renell, was fourteen, says Pamela Underwood. He hadn't gone very far, they say, when he stopped to help a woman. Then that car came screaming by. They shot my boy in the back of the head. In the back of the head. When they called to tell me my son had been shot, I kept telling them: Not my son. Not MY son. But it was my son.

One child lies on the floor in the suburbs, under the lights of a Christmas tree. Across town, another lies below the window ledge in a bathtub as gunfire erupts outside. Until a youngster somehow becomes a victim near suburban boundaries, the violence doesn't seem to touch an existence of manicured lawns and cable TV.

But black mothers of the inner city aren't the only ones who suffer.

Connie was fourteen. She was trying to be nice to the boy her aunt had taken in, says Cheryl Woods of Rocky Ridge. He was seventeen years old and kind of a "throwaway kid." He didn't know how to take it because she was nice. When she told him she just wanted to be friends, he wanted more. He was upset, and then he shot her; he killed her. I was angry with God for a long time. But my six-year-old told me that after what he did to Connie, her body wouldn't work anymore and there was no place for her to go but to heaven.

In poor areas, pride denies the problem. Things are blown out of proportion by a racist, class-oriented media, some believe. But there is no exaggeration. Alabama's violent crime rate went up three percent between 1990–1994. If you exclude violent crime in Birmingham from the calculation, the state rate would have dropped six percent.

Omarfio Houston Wiggins was my son, Betty Wiggins says. He graduated from Ramsay Alternative School with an advanced diploma and got his barber's license at age seventeen so he could earn money for college. He was so happy when he finally made it into Auburn. He was in great spirits when he came home from school for a holiday. They found him in his automobile downtown with a friend. Both dead. He was shot six times.

City Hall says we have to look to neighborhood cooperation to control crime. But people also need real leaders, not leaders who tell them to lead themselves. Nothing will help lower the crime rate like an aggressive, well-staffed police department. Nothing else will make good people who are most at risk safe.

Instead of praise, however, too many of the mothers at the podium tell of officers who were rude, of investigators who would not keep them informed.

Ezekiel had a full-time job and had never been in trouble, says his mother, Annie Hall. But when they found him in his car with a bullet in his back, the policeman kept implying that he shouldn't have been out wandering the streets at night. I told the officer that wasn't so; that Ezekiel had to have been shot in the daytime. He wouldn't believe it, though it later turned out to be true. Ezekiel was nineteen, but all of his life he had been afraid of the dark. He couldn't go out in it alone.

All of us want to hide behind the belief that there is some telltale flaw, some character trait, something—anything—that marks the victims. The truth is more random and more horrifying.

My son, Cedeno Daniel, was a youth Sunday school superintendent for his church, Elaine Richardson says. He was all alone in the house when he heard someone breaking in. He managed to call 911—but before a response came it was too late. They could have taken everything I own. I wouldn't care. Why did they take my son?

The most damning denial of all is that the problem is so big, so complicated there are no practical solutions. "It's just not true," says one social worker. "If we put as much money and effort into planning how to tackle these problems as we're talking about putting into planning a domed football stadium, we would make a serious dent."

The line of suffering at Shades Valley Presbyterian Church compels that commitment. Too many young people are dying. Too many children's lives are being ruined. No matter what lines we draw in geography, class, and race, these are our young people and our community's worth will be judged by how well it protects and nurtures them. The long line of haunting memories and hollow voices must grow no longer.

Altha Jones, a stout grandmother in a beret and large-lens spectacles, cannot tell her story into the microphone. The words are too hard. Instead, she stares blankly at the metal table as her anguish comes out of the tape recorder. It tells of how her son, Robert, was slain on a spring night in June of 1994. Of how, in the midst of her grieving for him, her daughter, Aletha Terry, was gunned down in Elyton Village seven months later, the victim of a drive-by shooting. Neither killer has been caught.

I have a pain that is always there, the tape recording says. My daughter had three children. Now I have to raise them. It's not an easy job you have to go through when they shoot your children down. I don't sleep at night anymore. Many times, I get up and read my Bible until daybreak. It seems so hard, like nobody cares as long as it is not them. It bothers me dearly. It hurts me in my heart. Y'all help us mothers. Please help us. Please help us. Please. Help us.

III

Dixie's Broken Heart

Alabama has called itself the "Heart of Dixie State," and "Dixie's Broken Heart" became the name of an award-winning 1998 series written by Bailey Thomson for the *Mobile Press-Register*. Pieces from that series appear in various sections of this book. But "Dixie's Broken Heart" works well as the title of this section, in which Thomson and Casey address various ways in which state government has gone awry in Alabama. They write about the grip of special interests, and about the tendency of the legislature to postpone action on social issues until forced to confront them by the federal courts.

BAILEY THOMSON

A State in the Shadow
of Special Interests

August 16, 1998, *Birmingham News*

A visitor to Montgomery might stroll along Dexter Avenue and admire the Confederacy's columned birthplace or meditate at the Baptist church where Martin Luther King Jr. began his civil rights crusade. Each shrine complements the other in helping to explain why Alabama voters behave as they do. Like Faulkner's characters, Alabamians often view the present by the dim light of the past, particularly on the issue of race.

Arrayed around these holy places, however, are buildings that speak to the current state of politics. They house the special interests, great and small, that exercise much of the permanent power. Their offices surround the old Capitol and the State House as if laying siege to the elected government.

Our visitor, as he continues his walk, might stop to admire the imposing headquarters of the Alabama Education Association, or chance to see a helicopter land on the roof of the Business Council of Alabama. Such special interests can afford staffs of specialists to research issues and lobby the legislators. They can mobilize thousands of constituents to speak for or against some proposal. They amass war chests to reward or punish politicians during campaigns.

By contrast, our visitor may be disappointed as he tours the State House. Legislators share secretaries, and they scurry to meetings in cramped hearing rooms. Committees have some staff members to help draft and review legislation, but lawmakers usually depend upon lobbyists for information.

In some cases, legislators become virtual appendages of special interests. Consider, for example, connections to the education establishment.

In 1995, when the legislature considered Gov. Fob James's proposal for funding schools and colleges, twenty-eight legislators were drawing paychecks from public educational institutions. Another eighteen were married to educators. These forty-six households represented a third of the legislature. Moreover, the speaker pro tem of the House was a community college president, as was one of his colleagues.

This overwhelming presence helps explain why the legislature maintains a separate trust fund for education, which receives the largest share of tax dollars. But earmarking of money does not stop with schools. In fact, trust funds have so proliferated that the legislature and governor have discretion over only about eleven percent of state spending.

This restriction of representative leadership is a legacy of Alabama's 1901 constitution. The document, with its 615 amendments, is notorious for weakening government.

Despite the deficiencies of its government, Alabama manages to attract many good people to fill offices. And since the 1960s, governing has become more democratic. For example, it may surprise our visitor to the capital to learn that more than seven hundred blacks serve as elected public officials—a result of civil rights victories won in Montgomery, Selma, and other battlefields.

But the fruits of reform have been disappointingly few for whites and blacks alike. Opportunists know how to exploit divisions of race and class, and they play upon voters' distrust of government. They also encourage citizens to put private gain ahead of public good.

The consequences of such politics are evident in three aspects of public life: weak local government, unfair taxation, and poor education. In each case, a failure to substitute better governance owes in no small part to special interests, who have thwarted reformers and manipulated citizens' fears and gullibility.

By no means, however, do these interest groups fight under one banner. They frequently battle one another over proposed changes, as when business groups supported school reforms against the opposition of the teachers' union. But under such confusing and divisive conditions, the advantage typically belongs with those who can exploit the political system's preference for the status quo.

This warped system allows certain interests to avoid paying fair taxes. For example, the state has the nation's lowest rates for property taxes, which generally fall upon those who are best able to pay. By contrast, Alabama socks its poor citizens with heavy sales taxes—even on their groceries and nonprescription drugs. The Public Affairs Research Council at Samford University found that citizens making less than $15,000 in 1994 paid nine percent of their income in state and local taxes, while those making more than $100,000 paid about seven percent.

Unfortunately, the state's regressive system seems impervious to reforms that might give poor people relief. A task force that Gov. Guy Hunt appointed in 1991 labored to devise a more equitable plan. But to no avail. Farm and timber interests resisted property tax increases, while other groups also clamored for protection. Reformers advocating fair taxation found themselves drowned out in Montgomery, while their opponents could always raise the specter of runaway taxes to frighten voters.

Not that citizens are entirely blameless for this shameful mess. Voters regularly reject fair school taxes. And racist appeals continue to resonate with a large part of the electorate. Alabama's much lamented failure to elect a "New South governor" owes in no small measure to a political culture that plays to the worst side of voters.

One recent governor, however, did attempt to hoist the colors of the vaunted New South. Jim Folsom Jr., who succeeded the disgraced Hunt following the latter's removal from office, mounted the most ambitious attempt by any modern governor to improve Alabama's schools.

As other governors had done before him, Folsom could say the courts were forcing him to act. A Montgomery circuit judge had ruled that the great disparities of funding from one school district to the next violated the state's constitution. Still, Folsom seemed motivated to help ordinary people improve their lot, much as his father had tried to do when he was governor in the 1940s and '50s. Unlike Big Jim Sr., however, the son moved comfortably among business leaders—the very kind of people his daddy had dismissed as "Big Mules." These business leaders helped persuade him that Alabama was overdue for school reform. Folsom responded with an ambitious plan that demanded higher performance in return for about $1 billion more in spending.

Folsom allied himself with a reform group called A-Plus. Its speakers stumped the state, telling audiences that Alabama's public schools dwelt in the basement when it came to most important measures, from funding to test scores. They met a fierce counterattack from the conservative activist group Eagle Forum, which rejected the reformers' emphasis on measuring school performance in terms of outcomes. In extreme cases, opponents painted the plan in satanic colors, seeing a vast conspiracy to strip away traditional values and local control.

In reality, many legislators needed no excuses to oppose school reform. They took their cues from Paul Hubbert, head of the Alabama Education Association. He and his union preferred to interpret reform as meaning guaranteed pay for teachers, smaller classroom enrollments, and better benefits on top of what already was a Cadillac package.

Our visitor to Montgomery might find other examples that show why many thoughtful Alabamians are dissatisfied. The state's higher education system, beset with political intrigue and inefficiency, squanders millions to provide easy access for students, yet it seldom wins high marks for quality. Alabama's prison system gains international notoriety for chain gangs, yet struggles to house a growing inmate population. And even on routine matters of governance, such as budgeting for capital projects, Alabama resists progressive methods.

Such complaints, to be sure, are part of an old story. Alabama has never known any golden age. From the state's earliest experiences with democracy, when politicians eagerly sought some issue or "hobby" to exploit, to the current obsession with religious practices in public schools, statecraft usually has placed a distant second to political opportunism.

What has changed, however, are the stakes. The price of ineffective government becomes intolerable as Alabama's citizens confront economic competition, and not just from other states but from all corners of the globe.

Like our fictional visitor in Montgomery, Alabamians observe the facade of state government, with all its traditions and trappings. But thus far, they have not demanded that the powers behind the facade be accountable. Is it any wonder, then, that Alabama continues to live in its past, unable to learn from its mistakes and unwilling to trust leadership that might hold a beacon for the future?

RON CASEY

When Will Comedians' Jokes Not Be on Alabama?

April 25, 1997, *Birmingham News*

A TV station in Alabama is refusing to air the coming-out episode of Ellen because they don't think it's appropriate for family viewing. A spokesman for the station said, "Homosexuality is not a topic that two cousins should watch with their children."

Conan O'Brien said that about us recently on his late-night talk show.

I hate it. I hate that a state whose main sin is being full of poor, under-educated people becomes the butt of some smarmy comedian's jabs.

I hate it because we leave ourselves wide open for such treatment.

This is not a state of bad people. It is a state of bad leaders. We've got a governor who thinks more of keeping a no-new-taxes pledge than of helping the neediest children in Alabama—and he'll varnish over that astounding callousness by telling us how much he supports the Ten Commandments.

We've had governors in the past who thought more of convincing America we're all hayseed racists than of helping poor blacks and poor whites scratch a living out of a dirt-poor state.

Other Southern states have elected more progressive leaders. Alabama is held back by a devil's brew of obstacles:

1. Custom.

One of the things you see in other states that have good leaders is a chain reaction. Once you have one, the tradition builds on itself—say as in North Carolina, where Luther Hodges was followed as governor by Terry Sanford and James Hunt.

In Alabama, where 900,000 adults lack a high school education, people win on gut-level issues, not intellectual arguments. In the 1950s and 1960s, the issue was race. In the 1970s, George Wallace had us hating those big utility companies. After that we hated the Baxley-Graddick feud. Now we're on the Ten Commandments.

None of those issues ever gave a poor person a job.

Few of those governors we elected on emotion had any vision of what the state needed over the long term. Those who did lacked the political ability to do much about it. Through many administrations the governor acted as if his main job after election was to dispense patronage.

2. Lack of diversity.

A poll run by this newspaper a few years back said that twenty-five percent of the respondents had never left Alabama. We have one of the highest percentages of native residents of any state. Of all the people who claim church membership here, sixty-seven percent say they belong to the Southern Baptist Convention.

There's nothing wrong with being a Southern Baptist. I was raised as one. Nor is there anything wrong with being a native resident.

It does mean we have not had many outside influences. We are who we are, and the only tradition of politics we know about has been disgraceful.

Even when we've had new political elements added, they've tended to mimic the old. Black political groups that came to power after voting rights legislation, for instance, simply copied the patronage model.

3. Mechanics.

A professor friend of mine says he hasn't done any research on this yet, but he thinks there's a difference in how campaigns are run.

In other states, there's a sort of natural winnowing out process. Economic interests don't give a lot of money to backward candidates. They are out of the race early. Here, campaign money folks mostly cover their rear ends.

It stems from the fact that for decades, the state legislature has taxed based on one rule: find the weakest guy in sight and mug him. That encouraged special-interest groups to become extraordinarily strong political players.

Instead of a variety of economic interests throwing money, we have four political parties—the Alfa party, the trial lawyers' party, the AEA party, and the Business Council of Alabama. In recent years, they have often (but not always) picked candidates on two criteria: (1) He can't be a mental giant or he may give us an argument and (2) he must look good on television. Then they toss a lot of money at him.

So are we stuck always with being the butt of jokes; with having governors who thump the Bible while they kill children's programs?

Not necessarily.

You could get a realignment of those strong interest groups. A coupling of business and education people would be a powerful combination.

New forces could alter things. Half the people in this state—women—have been all but excluded from decision-making.

Or other forces could alter their thinking. Why, for instance, does the Christian Coalition not see that in a state with the most regressive taxes in the Union, tax reform is a moral issue? Or that proper funding for poor schoolchildren is?

At a Leadership Alabama conference a few weeks ago, former Gov. Albert Brewer (one of our best chances ever for progressive leadership until Wallace beat him with a blatantly racist campaign) was asked what he wanted for Alabama. His answer:

A partnership to do the things that need to be done to build a state where everyone has a feeling of kindness and generosity and is willing to cooperate and work for the benefit of all of our people.

Amen. Then the joke would be on Conan O'Brien.

RON CASEY

Fishy Argument

November 23, 1993, *Birmingham News,* unsigned editorial

Monday was Alabama day in the *Wall Street Journal.*

First there was a report on the Leisure & Arts page about the Alabama-Auburn football game (Auburn won). Then, on the editorial page, a picture of our very own Alabama sturgeon.

The photo accompanied an impassioned editorial warning that the ugly fish soon will be "shutting down a good chunk of southern Alabama."

Help us! Rescue us from this terrible fate!

The *Journal* then went on to make a bunch of reasonably reasonable complaints about the Endangered Species Act and the (lack of) scientific evidence that the Alabama sturgeon is a distinct species or even still in existence. One of the strongest arguments was that the Endangered Species Act's "scattershot attempt to preserve everything defies any sensible attempt to make rational choices."

No huge gaps in logic there. We would add, in fact, that the species law's tendency to punish instead of reward people who have rare plants or animals on their property is misguided and dangerous.

But back to that initial point, that placing the Alabama sturgeon on the endangered list will soon shut down southern Alabama. It's a misinterpretation. It's an exaggeration. Whatever you want to call it, it ain't gonna happen.

The statement is based on assertions by the U.S. Fish and Wildlife Service that dredging the Alabama and Tombigbee rivers may harm the sturgeon. Businesses that depend on river traffic extrapolated that to mean all dredging will be halted if the sturgeon makes the list. They then got the U.S. Army Corps of Engineers to say that if all dredging is halted, the rivers will cease to be navigable within twelve months.

Fine. And if we had sturgeons swimming through our newsroom, we wouldn't be able to put out a newspaper.

But whatever happens to the sturgeon, shipping is not going to stop on the Alabama and Tombigbee rivers.

First of all, the Endangered Species Act allows for economics to play a role in deciding how to protect a species. Remember that big brouhaha about the snail darter endangered by the proposed Tellico Dam on the Tennessee River? Guess what—the dam got built.

More importantly, the people at the Fish and Wildlife Service admit they don't know a whole lot about the Alabama sturgeon, but they figure its habits are similar to those of the Gulf sturgeon—a species on the "threatened" list, one step below endangered. In a 1992 letter to the Corps of Engineers, the head of Fish and Wildlife's Daphne office wrote that the Corps' dredging has "no effect" on the Gulf sturgeon.

To be sure, the Fish and Wildlife Service is sending mixed messages. And the Alabama companies that use the rivers are perfectly justified in looking out for their interests, although it would be good if they could be less shrill about it.

But to make the sturgeon a national cause celebre, the next spotted owl, is the rankest ichthyogoguery. Those who are doing it are interested not in Alabama's economy, but in finding a convenient blunt instrument with which to batter the Endangered Species Act.

BAILEY THOMSON

Chains Rattle from a Brutal Past

March 5, 1995, *Mobile Press-Register*

I spent the summer of my seventeenth year as a laborer on a surveying crew. Often during that time, I worked alongside prisoners, who were assigned to road duty. Their camp, enclosed by barbed wire, was next to the office where we gathered every morning before heading to our next job.

On some days our crew surveyed the right-of-way for a new road. That meant I had to whack at undergrowth with a bush ax so the boss could peer through the little telescope on his transit and tell another fellow where to drive a stake. Other days, we worked shirtless on construction projects, showing equipment operators how high to pile their dirt as they prepared a new road for pavement.

When we worked on the road jobs, the convicts frequently joined us. Dressed in prison white and free to walk around, they did a lot of shoveling and similar hard labor, but they endured about the same conditions as the hired help. At noon, we crew members would dig out our lunch boxes and find a shady tree. The convicts, meanwhile, ate pork and beans and cornbread heated in cans over fires fueled with gasoline. We all went home tired.

Those experiences came to mind when Gov. Fob James recently announced plans to revive chain gangs in Alabama—a sight that predated my surveying career. The prison system has spent $17,000 for three hundred sets of leg irons, and it appears ready to make such gangs a regular part of its program. Interstate motorists will soon see felons shackled to one another working along the roadside.

There is nothing wrong, in principle, with putting convicts to work on the highways. Felons owe the state for their keep. Besides, idleness breeds danger in a prison, where time moves at half-speed and violence flares easily.

But reviving the chain gangs—with all the negative stereotypes they suggest about the South—is a strange policy indeed for a modern governor, particularly one in Alabama. Why? Because the state has a notorious history for violating human rights. Indeed, few episodes can rival its mistreatment of convicts, who for many decades were little better than slaves as the state leased them to mines, turpentine camps, and other brutal places.

Alabama was the last to abandon this practice. For decades, reformers fought the system and the vested interests that profited from its misery. It took a case arising out of Mobile to shame the legislature into accepting Gov. Bibb Graves's demand that convict leasing end.

A prisoner named James Knox, sentenced for forging a $30 check, died at the Flat Top Prison Mine in 1924. The attorney general later discovered that Knox had a heart attack after being beaten and dipped in hot water. The investigation produced national outrage against Alabama. It also gave ammunition to reformers, including many church people, who condemned convict leasing as barbaric. Finally, following the leadership of Governor Graves, the legislature abolished the system in 1928.

Along with the symbolic issue that a revival of chain gangs raises, there is a practical matter. Putting dangerous convicts to work outside the prison creates a possibility that some might escape.

The convicts whom I worked alongside generally could be trusted. They didn't run when they got the chance, so the guards didn't have to shackle them. They just wanted to serve their time and get out of there.

Medium-security felons present a different picture. If one of them cuts loose, the governor will have to answer for it. Voters get touchy over such incidents. Many may applaud James now for bringing back the chain gangs, but they would likely turn on him if a convict hurts someone.

The real difficulty with chain gangs, however, is that they belong to an earlier, dark chapter of the state's history, when shackled convicts were commonly brutalized. There is no escaping that image, particularly after movies such as *Cool Hand Luke* made chain gangs a metaphor for inhumanity. Does a smart governor really want to court such controversy, particularly when his industry hunters try so hard to project an upbeat image for Alabama?

Whether or not he's ready to admit it, Governor James has inherited a severe education problem that will take a lot of money and leadership to fix. Many of the state's nearly 20,000 inmates might be elsewhere had they received more attention as children. Yet school reform appears dead in the water, while the rest of the country reads about our new prison policy. Just as we were the last state to abolish convict leasing, we are now the first to revive the chain gangs.

As the warden in *Cool Hand Luke* might say: What we have here, Governor, is a failure to communicate.

RON CASEY

Prayer and Protest

November 13, 1997, *Birmingham News,* unsigned editorial

In 1870, Mark Twain wrote an essay called "Illegal Persecution of a Boy" that is relevant to the controversy in some Alabama schools now.

A "well-dressed boy on his way to Sunday school" was arrested for stoning a Chinese man, Twain explains. Then he goes through a lengthy recitation of all that state leaders in California had done over the years to demean and discriminate against Chinese Americans. And he wonders why the boy was even arrested: "Everything conspired to teach him that it was a high and holy thing to stone a Chinaman, and yet he no sooner attempts to do his duty than he is punished for it."

State leaders are called that because they are supposed to be our guides.

Instead of suspending children around this state who have boycotted classes in protest of a court decision on religion in schools they do not understand, we ought to look toward Gov. Fob James for the blame.

James, who threatened to call out the National Guard to keep a lawful court order from being implemented in the case of a judge who wants to display the Ten Commandments in his courtroom.

James, who says the Bill of Rights doesn't apply in Alabama.

James, who, when told that sixty students had walked out of Sardis school in protest of this latest order, said, "I don't blame them at all . . . When the depth, the arrogance, the meanness of this order sets in and people understand it for what it is, I would not be surprised at what may happen."

One of the governor's spokesmen (not the governor himself) issued a statement Saturday urging students to end protesting.

But by then the damage of three years' worth of a governor who attacks religion rulings with all the bluster and rebelliousness Alabama governors used to reserve for segregation had been done.

How much more productive will be Attorney General Bill Pryor's approach.

Pryor has urged children and parents not to protest, but instead to wait for his appeal to run its course. It's a good appeal.

U.S. Judge Ira DeMent's ruling, despite the governor's claims, was neither mean-spirited nor arrogant. The judge had been asked by defendants in a religion-in-the-schools case to provide guidance on a handful of issues they found unclear.

He did, trying to cite rulings in his circuit so that school boards would have appropriate information about what could and could not be allowed. We don't agree with everything DeMent says. But according to Donald Sweeney, attorney for the defendants, "Throughout this case, Judge DeMent has gone to great lengths to express how much he respects and supports religious expressions."

Attorney General Pryor thinks DeMent's order may have been too broad and is challenging it because he thinks recent court rulings weren't taken into consideration.

That's fine. The idea is to come up with the best possible plan for allowing individual expression of religious beliefs.

No school should proselytize for any religion. But neither should an individual student or group of students be denied their right under the First Amendment (which, contrary to James, does apply here) to worship.

Pryor's well-reasoned argument in court has a better chance of finding that balance than James's demagoguery.

BAILEY THOMSON

Bring Back the Bands

October 2, 1994, *Mobile Press-Register*

My third-grade teacher, Mrs. Thelma McKee, liked to clip pictures and stories from the *Birmingham News* so that we would know the candidates running for governor. There were about a dozen seeking the Democratic nomination, which in 1958 was tantamount to election.

Politics had personal meaning, even to us youngsters. I remember walking home one day and seeing a crowd of mostly older boys hurling sticks and rocks at a campaign poster somebody had nailed to a tree. Their parents obviously supported somebody else and hadn't bothered to explain the principle of free speech.

Similar passions erupted when the candidates roared through town on campaign stops. Large crowds turned out to hear them and to marvel at the country singers and other entertainment they brought along.

On the night young George Wallace spoke at the National Guard armory, my father and I were sitting near the front. Minnie Pearl warmed up the crowd, letting go her famous "Howww-deeee" into the microphone. My mother later reported that the Methodists heard the screech during choir practice a half mile away. The fightin' judge himself mesmerized us with the best speech I'd ever heard, causing my father to shake his hand warmly afterward and worry about his own candidate's chances against this gifted newcomer.

Wallace didn't win that time, but he placed a strong second to John Patterson. Thereafter, Wallace campaigns became a quadrennial part of our lives. Even after I was old enough to understand how the feisty little man played to people's fears about integration and other changes sweeping our society, I still went to hear him. He was the best of the bunch on his feet, speaking from a boxer's crouch and punching the air as he verbally jabbed at pointy-headed bureaucrats and liberal reporters.

I can't say exactly when the fun went out of politics, because I wasn't thinking about it at the time. In fact, I was covering campaigns myself and eager to show my sophistication about opinion polls, PACs, and other paraphernalia of modern politicking. But one day, I realized that kids probably didn't hear many politicians anymore from the stump. For that matter, they probably didn't declare their political allegiance with the kind of passion that once drove my schoolmates and me to shoving matches on the playground. Indeed, teachers might be satisfied nowadays if their students simply admit to watching political ads on television.

I was reminded last spring of what we've lost when I stumbled upon one of the gubernatorial candidates at Mobile's Bienville Square. He was buttonholing everybody he saw, including several bored policemen. Recognizing a journalist, he rushed over to grab my hand, apparently grateful for a familiar face. What had happened, I wondered, to the days when a candidate could attract a crowd just by pulling up in his motor caravan and having his musicians play a few chords? Gone. All gone, and we're the poorer for it.

A colleague asked me the other day if I had ever seen a duller governor's race. In fact, he added, does anybody even know there's one going on? Here it is nearly a month after Labor Day, when things were supposed to start, and the biggest news is how many millions of dollars Gov. Jim Folsom has raised to pay for his media campaign. There's little talk of issues, other than speculation about how the various political action committees manage to hide the money they slip to Folsom and other candidates.

An interesting paradox looms. As the stakes grow larger in the outcome of such elections, the public pays less attention to the candidates. This gubernatorial contest likely will determine whether Alabama overhauls its school system, as Folsom wants, or settles for tinkering, as James suggests. It could even point to a new state constitution, which Folsom advocates, or divert the state's energies into preserving the status quo, which seems to suit James. So where are the fiery debates? Where are the impassioned voters? Where is the campaign?

We in the press are partly to blame for this political torpor. We have played inside baseball with the political consultants, the pollsters, and all the other "professionals" who manipulate politics. We have strained to learn their lingo, listened to their off-the-record gossip, and even let them influence the "spin" we put on coverage. In effect, we have joined the image makers, sharing the mysteries and even the cynicism of their trade.

The voters, however, don't seem to care for such sophistication. In fact, an alarmingly high percentage of them believe that the system doesn't work or it surely doesn't work for them. Politics just doesn't make much sense anymore.

Well, it ought to make sense. Somehow, those of us who want responsive government have to help coax voters back into public life. They need to feel they're part of the process again, and not just raw numbers for the computers to crunch. That's why I would trade the whole pack of spin doctors and pollsters for a single hillbilly band and a crowd on a courthouse square listening to a candidate. I might not like what the speaker was saying, but at least there would be a real person standing up there, as opposed to a fuzzy, warm television image.

Funny, but I can still visualize most of those candidates on Mrs. McKee's bulletin board. I can even associate the faces of certain classmates with each of those names: Wallace, Faulkner, Patterson . . . They're part of a childhood experience that bears little resemblance to what passes for politics today.

RON CASEY

We've Endured Enough

August 31, 1990, *Birmingham News*

My daddy was a Primitive Baptist from Clay County. If I heard him say it once, I heard it a hundred times, an old saw from his church's belief in predestination.

"What can't be cured, must be endured."

If you had to pick a motto for the state of Alabama, that might be it.

I got to thinking about that as we worked on the series running on this page this week: "What they won't tell you about your taxes."

Another thing they won't tell you doesn't fit neatly into a category. It has to do with the nature of the people being taxed.

If you look at the hard numbers—the shortage of money for education, the shortage of money for basic human services—the impression is that there is also another shortage in Alabama: of compassion.

It's not so. The people of this state are as warm as a dinner-on-the-ground re-union.

If they're not hot to put more money into state services or education, it's be-cause their own life experiences place those things in the category of "luxuries."

Those whose parents sweated out the Great Depression behind the south end of a north-bound mule—when the average income in Alabama was $135—don't really think someone making close to $12,000 a year classifies as poor.

But that's the federal poverty level now.

The guy who had to quit school in the ninth grade to help his family earn a living, and went on to become a stripe-collar supervisor, doesn't really see the need for a formal study of "The Love Song of J. Alfred Prufrock."

But tell most of those same people a family down the street is in need, and they'll be there with an offer to help. Tell them a niece is graduating from high school, and they'll be first in line, with chest out and graduation present in hand.

The contradiction comes from decades of politicians telling those people the things that "can't be cured" are etched in stone. "We're just a poor state" is the ready answer to why we can't do something other states have done.

Human nature makes you low-rate things you can't have. If you can't have well-funded schools anyway, formal education becomes not nearly as important as "the school of hard knocks."

If you can't even keep the roads paved, then giving "handouts" to "people who ought to be working" is nonsense. (The mind closes out the possibility that many of them can't work or that the "handout" is probably only around $120 a month.)

We are a poor state. But we're not that poor. That kind of talk is just an age-old elixir from sideshow men who care more about getting elected than getting something done.

We may not ever have the most expensive schools in the country. But that doesn't mean we can't have the best schools—if we give them money they need and grab the governor, legislature, and educators by the scruff of the neck and demand it.

We may not ever have the best funded services. But we can have better services by making those goldbricks in our tax system pay up and by refusing to sell our God-given resources on the cheap.

The state of Alabama isn't some far-off, uncontrollable thing. It's us. It can be what we want it to be.

We have endured plenty, thank you. Come January, when the new governor and legislature take office, we ought to make sure that they start curing.

RON CASEY

"Alabama Is for Players"

February 2, 1996, *Birmingham News*, unsigned editorial

"Alabama is for Players."

We don't know how well that'll go over. But the Alabama Development Office this week unveiled the new slogan, which will be used in national advertising to attract new industry to the state.

It sounds like something Retirement Systems of Alabama CEO David Bronner might come up with to lure golfers to the RSA's Robert Trent Jones Golf Trail. Or a campaign Milton McGregor would offer if he'd ever been able to get casino gambling through the Alabama legislature. Or perhaps if all the colleges and universities with athletic programs got together for a joint recruiting campaign.

Actually, the "player" in the new ADO slogan describes people in business who have significant influence, according to John Eighmey, a University of Alabama advertising professor.

The slogan is meant to appeal to the egos of businesspeople looking to relocate or start up new operations. But is this the perfect statement about our state? After it finishes the "Alabama is for Players" campaign, the ADO can continue with a whole series of ads based on the "Alabama is for . . ." theme.

Alabama is for Prayers (we need all we can get.) Alabama is for Special-Interest Groups. Alabama is for Chain Gangs. Alabama is for Out-of-State College Students. Alabama is for Multimillion-Dollar Civil Lawsuit Judgments.

RON CASEY

The Problem Is in Who that "Somebody Else" Is Likely to Be

May 29, 1992, *Birmingham News*

"Anna's not down here," the neighbor's voice was nervous over the phone. "I sent her home for supper several minutes ago."

It was just about dark, and my four-year-old daughter was missing.

There was a hard rush of adrenalin. There was a brick in the pit of my stomach.

It took only about five minutes of frantic effort to find her. Running home from the back yard of her best friend's house two doors down, she stopped off to visit another neighbor.

But every parent knows that sick feeling. For the vast, very lucky majority of us, it quickly goes away.

The question is: why should it?

We all react the same way to clear, imminent danger to our children. Why don't we have that same reaction to the dangers—just as real and just as threatening—more distant?

Somebody will do something about them, we think. Will they?

My four-year-old already is in debt $16,000. So is my eight-year-old. So is every man, woman, and child in the United States.

That's about the per-person share of Uncle Sam's $4 trillion national debt.

In a year when the federal budget is a record-breaking $400 billion in the red, much of the talk in this presidential race is about how to spend the "peace dividend" from a cutback in military spending due to the end of the Cold War.

What company $4 trillion in the hock would pay anyone a "dividend"?

Much of the talk in the congressional races from incumbents will be about how much money they were able to bring home to their districts. They'll tell us about bringing home the bacon because that usually sizzles with voters.

Yet, next year the most expensive item in the federal budget won't be military spending, poverty programs, or Social Security.

It will be interest on the national debt.

Most of our parents struggled through the Great Depression and the dark uncertainties of World War II. A hallmark of their generation was sacrificing to make life better for their children than it had been for themselves.

The hallmark of our generation is going to be a pile of unpaid bills, because we refused to sacrifice. Somebody else should do something about it.

We live in a nation in which the average fourth-grader now reads less than five pages a day and does less than thirty minutes of homework, but watches at least three hours of television.

And Alabama is one of the most undereducated states in the nation.

We give our children less money to get an education than almost any other state. We don't test teachers before they get into the classroom, and have one of the toughest tenure laws in the country to protect them once they get a toehold there.

Alabama school systems went into debt $43 per child last year just to keep classes going after budget shortfalls. This year many of them are out of money and out of borrowing power. Already marginal schools will lay off teachers and shorten their terms.

Our recent legislative session voted to raise $128 million more every year for highway building. It reformed our workers' compensation system, one of the governor's top priorities.

But it did nothing about schools.

The governor says their money problems are "serious, but it's happened before" and it's just something we have to live with.

Maybe somebody else will do something about it.

Still, bad as those situations are, they're not the worst legacy we're leaving our children. We're poisoning their government, too.

Government no longer is seen as a positive force in our lives. It is gridlock and greed run by second-rate people who couldn't hold a job anywhere else. It can do nothing *for* us, only *to* us.

That kind of attitude feeds on itself. If you expect only gridlock, that's what you'll get. If government is a negative, the main concern is to defend yourself against it, not force it to work better. If government office is for second-rate people, why should first-rate people run?

We don't want to sacrifice to ease the crushing debt piling ever higher on the federal government.

We don't want to sacrifice to give our children a first-rate education.

And the bald truth is that we hold on to such attitudes about government because that's easier than admitting we don't want to sacrifice the time and effort as citizens it will take to recapture it.

Maybe somebody else will do all those things.

What ought to give us a continuing sickness in the pits of our stomachs is that the somebody else is likely to be the four-year-old playing in the yard today.

BAILEY THOMSON

Our New Century

October 17, 1998, *Mobile Press-Register,*
conclusion to "Dixie's Broken Heart" series

On the eve of the twentieth century, one hundred years ago, Alabamians looked confidently upon a dawning New South.

A vanquished people no more, they had trod the road to reunion. Their young men even fought alongside sons of Yankees to free Cubans from Spanish tyranny, while their statesmen in Congress, such as Sen. John Morgan, helped shape what would become the American Century.

Although many Alabamians were poor, they lived in a rich state. To the north, the Tennessee River watered fertile valleys. To the south, a splendid port welcomed commerce. A belt of black soil girded the state's middle, while a mountain range from the east deposited coal, iron ore, and limestone, the raw materials for Vulcan's forge.

No matter how tumultuous its past, Alabama seemed poised to fulfill the prophecies of boosters such as Atlanta editor Henry Grady, who saw a New South rising from the Civil War's ashes. And as the South rose, Alabamians expected their state to soar also into this new era of prosperity and enlightenment.

At least that was the dream a century ago.

In our time, we behold as did our ancestors a rich and promising land, but one that has changed almost beyond recognition. Modern cities have developed, along with universities and industries, so that Alabama's urban places now resemble those of its former conqueror. In the countryside, the farmer is mostly gone, replaced by the long-distance commuter, traveling highways that bind our civilization.

In the haste to exploit this bountiful land, however, we have often left it scarred and cut over. We have been careless with pollution, unwilling to address its damage out of fear that cleaner air and water might cost jobs. More recently, we have failed to manage runaway growth, which sprawls into rural areas with costly abandon.

Likewise, we have not cultivated a responsive democracy. Too often, the majority has forsaken political wisdom for the demagogue's rant. Without vision, our state perishes under the rule of special interests, who buy influence with political contributions.

But the democratic spirit has a remarkable resilience. It draws its strength not from rank or privilege but from the noble calling of citizenship. Once aroused and properly armed with powerful ideas, citizens form the greatest army the world has seen.

This week, we examined in this space five good ideas from our neighboring states. We sought to learn how these states have improved their civic life. None of them has met with unqualified success, and sometimes reforms require a generation to show results. But in important and inspiring ways, these neighbors have laid a foundation for the next century.

Let us briefly review some of their accomplishments:

South Carolina has pushed democracy down to the grass roots by allowing counties to govern themselves under home rule. Local government now has tools to manage sprawling, costly growth and to protect residents from threats such as corporate hog farms and junkyards.

North Carolina has made good teaching central to reforming its schools. The state encourages and rewards achievement, while intervening to counter failure. The state seeks not only to improve its teachers but also to encourage bright and dedicated people to enter the profession.

Florida has put children at the top of its agenda, investing heavily in preschool programs that encourage later success. As Gov. Lawton Chiles proclaims, education begins at gestation, and his leadership has taught Floridians the common sense of building healthy young bodies and inspiring inquisitive minds.

Mississippi has created a rational and economical system of community colleges, each working in tandem with the others to provide academic and vocational preparation. Through special tax districts, citizens help support their local campuses, contributing to their success rather than merely benefiting from their presence.

Louisiana has undergone a virtual civic renewal, reversing its plunge into corruption and despair. A citizens' organization inspired voters to create a new public agenda, one that would show the way out of the political wilderness.

These achievements show how motivated citizens can move mountains. When will we in Alabama do the same?

Alabamians often bemoan the fact that our state, virtually alone within the region, has never elected a New South governor. Since North Carolina's Terry Sanford provided the model of such enlightened and pragmatic leadership in the early 1960s, state after state has found governors in the same mold. By contrast, Alabama has mostly elected men who lifted their fingers to test the wind rather than thrusting out their chins to lead.

It's hardly a surprise, then, that many public schools teeter on failure. Children of working families lack decent health care. Colleges resist rational governance. Ugly sprawl devours our countryside. The shameful list goes on. And still we do not learn. Too often, our political choices remain a lesser of two evils, rather than competing visions of greatness. Such is the dilemma with our gubernatorial election next month:

Don Siegelman, the Democrat, presents himself as a moderate alternative. Yet he is strictly an old-school politician who cozies up to special interests that have stuffed his campaign account.

As lieutenant governor, Mr. Siegelman presided over the Alabama senate for four years. During that time, he blocked or failed to support good ideas that would have moved Alabama forward. The legislature did not reform the public schools. It did not fix the unfair tax system. It did not close loopholes in campaign finances. It did not wring a settlement or higher taxes from big tobacco companies. It did not rein in runaway civil-justice awards. The list goes on.

Yet Fob James, the Republican, is no answer, either. If anything, he might act even zanier once he is reelected and cannot succeed himself.

Already, Mr. James has attempted to liberate Alabama from compliance with the Bill of Rights, while resurrecting chain gangs, Confederate flags, and threats of resistance to federal authority. Is this the direction we want to go—backward? Mr. James would take us there if given an opportunity. These reasons explain why this newspaper chooses not to endorse in the gubernatorial election. Neither Mr. Siegelman nor Mr. James has shown himself to be worthy of high office, although thoughtful voters must choose between them.

We have stumbled to the crossroads of century's end, with too little to show for such a long journey. It is not enough, however, to bemoan lost opportunities. We must raise expectations for public life and hold politicians to a high civic standard. Only then can Alabama's democracy aspire to a politics of hope and accomplishment.

In Alabama, we can lag behind our neighbors, or we can stride forward with good ideas of our own. It is a decision we dare not delay, for things are moving too swiftly in the world for hesitation.

Indeed, bold action in one instance brought our state its finest recent accomplishment: a Mercedes assembly plant of global distinction. Yet we have not shown a similar willingness to raise the rest of Alabama to that level of excellence.

You can see the results along U.S. 11 in Tuscaloosa County, where the gleaming Mercedes plant meets crumbling Vance Elementary School. One image evokes a magic future, and the other a flawed past.

Perhaps some time in the next century, with the help of good ideas and strong leadership, these images will blend into a new Alabama, one worthy of being the Heart of Dixie. But we have miles to go before that happens.

Miles to go, and a broken heart to mend.

IV

Race

Ron Casey and Bailey Thomson were born into a rigidly segregated Alabama, and came of age during the civil rights movement, with some of its cataclysmic events happening near them in Birmingham and Tuscaloosa. Personal relations and experiences informed the progressive stands they took as writers, as did their careful study of state and regional history.

It's probably not surprising that Casey, in the top editorial writing position in Birmingham—a city seared by the Sixteenth Street Baptist Church bombing and demonstrations that preceded it—would write often and directly about race. Thomson did, too. This section concludes with Thomson's extended essay on Clarence Cason, a white Alabamian and journalism professor who in the 1930s made a cautious but still brave and eloquent depiction of Southern race relations in the book *90° in the Shade*.

RON CASEY

Why Go to the Moon If We Can't Get Along?

March 26, 1995, *Birmingham News*

The black woman's voice is pure and powerful. It hovers like a fresh night breeze over the singing of the choir and congregation of New Pilgrim Baptist Church.

Praise Him . . .

Praise His name . . .

For the white guy from Midfield on the podium about to "deliver the spoken word," it is a moment of revelation.

The "spirit," I'm sure, takes many forms. For me, it felt like a low-voltage electrical charge starting at my toes and wending slowly up through the bone marrow until it flowed out of the eyes as moisture.

If these folks keep singing, I am thinking, I will light up like a Christmas bulb.

I don't remember ever being more nervous about speaking somewhere than I was the day the secretary of the church called and asked me to talk at their annual Human Relations Day.

I've spoken to a lot of groups before, many of them groups of African Americans. But I had never spoken from a pulpit. You can't convince yourself that it's just a podium like any other. It is not.

At first, I had an easy out. I was supposed to be in New York on business that weekend, so I turned them down. But when I got my flight schedule, it turned out I could be back in plenty of time to do it.

Something kept tugging at me until I called the church and told them I could make it after all. Nonetheless, when I did, the panic attack began.

I spent only a small amount of time in New York speaking to a convention of college journalists. The rest of my stay I was holed up in a motel room fighting demons.

What in the world would I say? I kept hearing the booming voices of Abraham Woods and Martin Luther King Jr. and mentally comparing them to the nasal redneck drawl I've cultivated for forty-three years.

The morning before the service found me pacing back and forth on my patio (so Margie and the children wouldn't hear), going over it and over it one last time and trying to figure out something to do with my hands (because I'm awful about just putting them in my pockets when I talk).

When we all got to the tan, circular church on Goldwire, the first person to greet us was a big, older man whose wide smile and warm hand immediately began to melt my worries. Then there was a sea of friendly faces and hands put out to be shaken. A young man in a business suit showed me into the Rev. Nelson Smith's office, while Margie, my children, and our friend Carol found a seat.

The Reverend Smith looks like a man born to be a preacher—powerful, with gray hair and hands big enough to hold a whole congregation. He was absolutely amused at my nerves, I think.

We talked for a moment, then he ushered me through a side door as the opening prayer was ending. That revealed the semicircular auditorium of a large church about half-filled with worshipers.

There are differences between the Baptist church I grew up in and New Pilgrim. For starters, at my church there was a pulpit and a choir section behind it. At New Pilgrim, the choir is so large it lines two sides of the auditorium, sandwiching worshipers between two walls of music. Another is that worshipers continued to file in long after the service had begun until all the pews were full, and nobody seemed to care.

The service was less a lecture and more a celebration.

First a group of a half-dozen older men was called upon to perform spirituals in what the Reverend Smith called "the old way." Another member told me it was how they had been done in slave days, and the church tries to preserve the tradition. Their deep voices blended and diverged like the limbs of haunting oaks rooted in the humus of an ancient forest. Such music is more felt than heard.

A choir of maybe two dozen small children, which the Reverend Smith proudly referred to as "The Pastor's Choir," sang next. As I looked at the radiance of the young woman leading them, I believe we both shared the same thought—that a feast was being served.

Finally, the Reverend Smith said he wanted to "Praise Him," in a move I think was entirely improvisational. The hand-clapping spiritual began, and it seemed to last forever. Listening to it was like somebody had plugged your soul into an electrical socket.

When the Reverend Smith finally introduced me, he explained the rules of engagement. "Brother Casey," he said. "We 'amen' in this church. That means, if we like what you say, we say 'amen.' If we don't like what you say, we say 'Say what?' And if we really like what you say, we say 'Whoop.'"

My sole regret from last Sunday at New Pilgrim is that I never got a "Whoop." I took the pulpit no longer nervous that I might screw up. The genuine warmth of the congregation and each portion of the service had sucked it out of me gradually, like air from a tire. But I also knew there was no way anything I might say would match the fullness I felt.

It is a blur; like I wasn't talking, but somebody's voice was coming out. The voice talked about the awkwardness, confusion, and torment that have separated blacks and whites in the South as a vestige of segregation; about a state that has always tried to deal with its poverty by holding fast to what it has, rather than sharing to make something better; about how both blacks and poor whites have felt the sting from that.

I talked about how the effect of that disfranchisement and alienation could be summed up in a proverb from the Douay Bible which inspired the name of a famous book about Alabama: "And some there be which have no memorial; who perished as though they had never been; and who are become as though they had never been born; and their children after them."

That this is not what any of us want for our children. That though we can never live in unison, we must live in harmony—and what a joyful noise the people of Alabama will make when they do.

The applause was enough to let me imagine I wasn't the worst speaker they ever had. I was grateful for it. Then Reverend Smith responded, summing up in thirty seconds what I had been trying to fumble through for days.

That human relations are the most important problem we face. What does it matter if we can go to the moon, but can't get along with the person who lives next door to us?

Later, after another wonderful wave of hand-shaking concluded, we were invited to eat dinner. It was Alabama fried chicken, fresh vegetables, iced pound cake, and a lot of fellowship.

Somehow the topic turned to the rising debate over affirmative action programs and welfare reform. I wanted a lot more people on both sides of those issues to share that dinner table.

BAILEY THOMSON

Johnson Stood Like
Rock of Reason

August 1, 1999, *Birmingham News*

HALEYVILLE—The heat that enveloped mourners here Tuesday at Judge Frank M. Johnson's funeral was reminiscent of the hot summers of Selma and Montgomery and dozens of other civil rights battlefields. One had to live through those days and feel their passions to understand why the people who gathered around Johnson's grave revered his legacy.

As a federal judge, Johnson helped preserve Alabama's civic fabric during a dangerous time when many of its elected politicians were intent on defying federal authority. In those days, the white leadership reached an intellectual and moral impasse—unable to go forward and unwilling to recognize the sins of the past. Johnson cut through that confusion to uphold the essential qualities of a just and fair society. He read his Constitution and he took it seriously.

It is too easy to look back today and conclude that white Alabamians' reaction was an inevitable byproduct of their racist history. Leadership—or more precisely, the wrong kind of leadership—had a large role in bringing Alabama to the brink of collapse. We suffer even today from that failure of nerve and vision.

Images of police dogs and flying billy clubs sometimes obscure memory of a more hopeful chapter in Alabama's history. In fact, Alabama's voters from about the mid-1930s until the early '50s seemed most interested in economic justice, as small farmers and businesspeople joined workers in a powerful coalition. Significant change seemed not only desirable, but even possible.

Voters elected a succession of reformers who sought to give the little man a fair shake. The state's congressional delegation ranked among the South's most liberal and the nation's most influential. Among its leaders were Lister Hill, John

Sparkman, Carl Elliott, and Bob Jones. Some of these men had grown up them-selves in sharecropper shacks and knew firsthand the pinch of poverty.

In 1946, James E. Folsom shocked the state's political rings by winning the Alabama governorship with a promise of reform. He called for a fairly appor-tioned legislature, old age pensions, farm to market roads, an end to the poll tax, and better schools. People filled the auditoriums and town squares to overflow-ing, eager to hear his message.

Reactionaries in the Alabama senate, still a captive of the white planters and their industrialist allies, made a shambles of Folsom's first administration. Big Jim learned the hard way that getting elected and governing are two different things.

But Alabama's reformers in Congress enjoyed enormous success. They helped to expand rural health care and public housing, create a national student loan program, and promote other legislation to help common people. Sparkman ran as the Democratic vice presidential candidate in 1952, while his colleagues held key leadership positions.

Folsom returned to the governor's chair in 1954 with an even bigger mandate for economic and electoral reform. Alabama seemed poised to attack such lin-gering problems as an unfair tax system and a malapportioned legislature.

This time, Folsom gathered around him a more experienced team, who vowed to avoid the earlier mistakes. As before, the governor refused to engage in race-baiting. He chided conservatives from the plantation counties for their treat-ment of blacks: "If they had been making a living for me like they have for the Black Belt," he said, "I'd be proud of them instead of cussing and kicking them all the time."

Folsom called for a new state constitution. In particular, he attacked how the plantation counties, with their small white voting populations, controlled a dis-proportionate number of legislative seats, thereby denying equal representation to the more populous hill counties and urban areas. But Folsom, who stood six foot eight and electrified his listeners, failed to bring his gargantuan thirst and other weaknesses under control. Greedy hangers-on helped spoil his credibility just as Alabama desperately needed his leadership.

That same year of his second election, the U.S. Supreme Court struck down school segregation. As more decisions followed, many business and professional whites joined the Citizens' Council to resist integration, while their less cultured cousins donned white sheets. Fear and violence stalked the land.

Folsom sought a moderate course, hoping to hold his reform coalition to-gether. His enemies reviled him for not supporting the white resistance. When in 1956 a mob confronted a black student trying to enroll at The University of

Alabama, Folsom slinked around the outskirts of the crisis, unwilling or unable to affect events. Momentum shifted to those who would make race the controlling force behind Alabama politics.

Attorney General John Patterson, who succeeded Folsom as governor, courted the white extremists, having all but banished the NAACP from the state. Alabama veered down a dark and terrible road, as race trumped other issues and one by one the reform champions gave way to lesser men. Into this vacuum, unwittingly perhaps, strode Frank Johnson, who in November 1955 won an appointment from President Eisenhower to be a federal district judge in Alabama. Like Folsom and so many of the state's congressional delegation, Johnson hailed from a county that had been sympathetic to populist protest and demands for a fair shake. His father had even been one of those rare hill county Republicans who took Abraham Lincoln, rather than Jefferson Davis, as their hero.

This historic symmetry seems, in retrospect, almost providential. As many of Alabama's elected leaders began to exploit whites' prejudices, Frank Johnson upheld the noble constitutional principle that all men and women are created equal and deserving of protection from their government. A great contrast emerged: Alabama's elected leaders grew more cowardly and demagogic, while Johnson stood like a rock of reason and courage.

During those difficult years, some Southern federal judges tried to duck the integration crisis. Not Johnson. He joined those "unsung heroes," as his biographer called them, in carrying out the Supreme Court's unanimous 1954 ruling. His decisions rolled across the troubled land, outraging his fellow whites but comforting beleaguered blacks.

Beginning in 1955, he joined two other federal judges in ordering an end to segregated public transit systems. He went on to rule in landmark cases that all citizens deserved an equal right to vote. In some places such as Lowndes County just below Montgomery, not a single black had been allowed to register, although African Americans were in the majority.

Johnson's great nemesis was his law school classmate George Wallace, who after losing to Patterson in 1958 turned his back on the reform tradition and became the greatest demagogue of his era. Worse, Wallaceism was soon to infect the nation, tapping what historian Dan Carter calls the "politics of rage" among blue-collar whites.

Alabama is still recovering from the collective madness that Patterson and Wallace helped spread. The symptoms show when special interests join resentful whites to defeat bond issues for dilapidated public schools. They show when politicians wrap themselves in the Ten Commandments or the Confederate flag or some other symbol, rather than address real issues that might require courageous answers.

Fortunately, however, Alabama had Judge Johnson and other federal jurists to keep the ship of state aright. He issued the first court order to reapportion a state legislature, which evolved into the Supreme Court's famous one-person, one-vote decision. He integrated Alabama's state troopers. He cleaned up filthy, dangerous conditions in the state's mental institutions and prisons.

Many Alabama politicians publicly cursed him for such actions. But deep down the smart ones surely thanked God that this principled man would do the right thing when they wouldn't.

RON CASEY

The Wall between Black and White Fell, but the Rubble Remains

February 10, 1995, *Birmingham News*

My well-educated friend was talking to another woman about a long-ago acquaintance who once was a baby-sitter for both.

"Of course I remember her. I got mad at her once when I was a little girl and called her 'nigger.' Boy, did she straighten me out about that word and quick."

The look on her face was of admiration, not racism.

I tell the story because it seems to me that during Black History Month, one of the more interesting histories is the development of personal relationships between Southern blacks and whites over the past thirty years.

We Birmingham natives in our forties were born into a harshly segregated society. When the legal wall between the races was removed it was like two distant cultures peering at one another not knowing quite what to expect.

I heard Mayor Arrington tell a group of editorial writers last year that when he was growing up he didn't know there were different kinds of white people. It never occurred to him that there might be Italian white people or Irish white people. White people were all alike.

Of course they weren't. Growing up in Midfield in the 1950s and 1960s, I remember my family avoiding going to the shopping center on Friday night (our usual social event) because the "kluxers" or the states' righters were going to have a flat-bed truck rally. You didn't want to be involved with those people.

The injustice of segregation hit me theoretically at some point. But it didn't hit me personally until I got to know people on the other side of the wall.

I recall seeing the "Colored Only" water fountains and the "We Reserve the Right to Refuse Service to Anyone" signs, and not thinking about it much one way or another. That was the way things were.

But years later my friend Harold told me that in those days, his family had to plan trips well in advance, because black folks never knew where they might find a restaurant or a motel that would serve them.

My friend Ingrid brought flesh-and-blood reality to the fire hoses and police dogs in Kelly Ingram Park. She was listening to a group of whites at a seminar say we had to just let bygones be bygones. You don't understand, she told them, with a passion that stunned me. Those were my friends. They were children the same age as me; people I went to school with—nine, ten, eleven years old. They got beaten and bitten and knocked down with fire hoses. And nobody ever apologized.

I heard the Reverend Porter tell about boarding the train to Atlanta shortly after "integration." Each time the conductor would ask his destination and then point toward a car at the rear. He wasn't about to be treated that way anymore, though, so he always went the other way. One day the conductor asked what the heck was going on, explaining that all he was trying to do was get him to a comfortable car because he was a long-distance traveler. Sure enough, the car was more comfortable.

But I also heard Norm, who has two children, tell about working for weeks to make a sale to a rural city council, until someone pulled him aside. "The only reason I'm telling you this is because you're working so hard," he said. "There is no way a black will get this sale."

I heard a black elected official talk about working hard, too—for a political party because a party hack kept saying, "You help the party and the party will help you." When he announced he was going to run for a higher office, though, the response from the pol was: "Really. What does Joe Reed say about it?"

Just when I was beginning to think black political machines like Reed's were an anachronism, I heard about a candidate in this county who got so far ahead in a political race she decided to put her African American face (instead of just her name) on some ads. Her polls crashed in a week. She lost.

I remember my friend Bill, one of the brightest guys I know, telling me that what would really help race relations is to have someone, without mealy-mouthing, stand up and say, "I'm sorry. You were done wrong."

But I also remember an essay in C. Vann Woodward's *Burden of Southern History* about the awkwardness Southern whites feel in dealing with these issues because they are from a region which twice within a century put everything it had into losing the fight for the wrong cause.

When I went up to the podium to give a speech in a civic club a couple of years ago, I saw Leon in the third row. I hadn't seen him in years. I joked to the audience that he and I had gone to the same high school, the only difference was that they let me go to the prom. He laughed out loud.

After my speech, we talked for a while about what a long time ago that was and what a strange journey it had been. We weren't black or white, we were people who went to school together and had some bizarre memories to reminisce about. His capacity for forgiveness overcame my guilt.

The wall is gone. The rubble remains, though. It seems to me the way to clear it away is to try to be honest, to separate the misguided from the mean-spirited in our past, and to understand that the strange journey has been so much stranger for one group of resilient citizens who were not only separate but unequal.

RON CASEY

It's Time State Got
off Backs of the Poor

June 4, 1999, *Birmingham News*

I don't know Mr. Warren's history.

All I know is that the lady who used to live behind us had one of the best yards in the neighborhood, and Mr. Warren (who calls himself by a nickname) took care of it.

So I asked him to start tending ours. For years, he has come around not on any regular basis, just when the lawn really needs mowing or the leaves really need raking. He works all day trying to do a better-than-expected job. "That's when the people will hire you again," he says.

Mr. Warren is at least in his mid-sixties, and he is an African American.

Last week, I saw him walking along the street pushing a lawnmower. I thought he was taking care of a nearby lawn, but I was wrong.

His wife has Alzheimer's, he said. A few days before, he was trying to make a loud-mouthed young tough outside his house be quiet for her when they got into a verbal fight. That night his car—an early 1970s station wagon with two doors that didn't match anything else on it—was burned. So he pushes his lawnmower from job to job, all the way across Homewood if he has to, trying to make do.

The poor. When we think of that faceless group, many picture people who while away the hours buying beer and cigarettes with food stamps out of a welfare Cadillac.

The truth is, most of the poor are people like Mr. Warren. They work every day, but they don't make enough to rise above poverty. Instead of helping them, Alabama continues a century-old shell game.

Before the Civil War, much of the state's revenue came from taxes on slaveholders. When slaves were freed by the war, the state not only lost the revenue, but found itself with hundreds of thousands of new black residents it was supposed to provide services for out of an economy that had been smashed.

To oversimplify, the way we ultimately found to parcel out the scarcity was segregation. No group in Alabama would get very much from state services. Blacks would get least of all.

After all, they (and eventually poor whites, as well) couldn't vote.

When the Voting Rights Act passed, the state had to find another way. It continued the shell game, but with new victims:

Over the next several decades lawsuits would be filed against it for failure to provide anything above Third-World support for its mentally ill, its children in state custody or in state schools, and its prison inmates.

After all, none of them voted either. The results still haunt us.

It costs more to board a dog for a month than this state pays foster parents to keep a child.

If a family of three makes more than $65 a week, it is ineligible for Medicaid. That's the lowest cutoff in the country. That cuts 78,000 working Alabama parents out of help with health care.

Federal highway money coming into Alabama has increased by $200 million, yet poverty groups are struggling desperately to get just $4 million of that for public transit.

Of the $14 million the federal government would give Alabama to aid getting people off welfare and into work, this state has spent $20,000. We did not match the federal money.

We have the highest guard-to-prisoner ratio of any corrections system in the region. We spend less per inmate than any state in the union. What kind of rehabilitation is that supposed to buy?

And on top of all that, several studies have said Alabama's tax system is the most regressive in the country. It taxes the poor with a heavier burden than the affluent.

Such callousness was born when Alabama was one of the poorest states in the union. Now, however, we rank thirty-eighth in the nation in median family income.

Yet, we still collect the smallest General Fund revenues in the region. Why?

"Custom reconciles us to everything," said Edmund Burke.

We dehumanize the poor because it is easier than admitting there are some debts to be paid. In the process, our lack of investment in our own people costs us much more in the long run.

A huge percentage of those in our prisons and on food stamps never got an education past the primary grades. It would cost much less to educate them in decent schools.

People who don't have access to Medicaid show up in hospital emergency rooms rather than getting much less expensive care in regular doctor visits. When they can't pay, it raises the cost of health care for all of us.

Worst of all is the wasted potential. I think of a man like Mr. Warren and his work ethic. How far might he have gone had he lived in a state that was on his side rather than on his back?

RON CASEY

Look toward the Higher Ground

October 2, 1992, *Birmingham News*

"They're going to have a statue of police dogs down there, too?" said the agitated but friendly suburbanite over the barbecue grill. "I mean what did they want us to do? Shoot people?"

He was talking about a news story on the newly redone Kelly Ingram Park, with its statues saluting civil rights marchers.

I suspect a lot of whites will react that way to the park, and to the Civil Rights Museum going up across the street from it. What disturbs me is that it's understandable they would.

Probably more whites in Atlanta or New York know the full story of what happened in Kelly Ingram Park in 1963 than here. Our city's media did not do its job of reporting events to the people in the perspective deserved.

I have no qualms about making that statement, even if I am ambivalent about what it means. My inclination is to be harshly critical. But in 1963, I was twelve years old. I have no idea what kind of awful atmosphere people must have been operating in.

The problem we ought to deal with now is the residual effect. There is a great gulf of understanding between blacks and whites in Birmingham over what transpired.

Whites tend to see Kelly Ingram Park as a place where a civil disturbance broke out which was handled as humanely as possible. Blacks tend to see it otherwise. "I had friends in high school who were arrested, who were chased by those dogs," said a friend of mine a few months back. "It's personal."

What did happen?

Taylor Branch's meticulously researched book *Parting the Waters* offers the bare facts.

By the spring of 1963, the civil rights effort was running out of steam. A winter push in Albany, Georgia, hit Jell-O. There Police Chief Laurie Pritchett met demonstrators with the deadly weapon of peaceful coexistence. There was no confrontation, and very little news.

Birmingham officials decided to follow the same plan, with one addition: demonstrations here would be confined to the city's black areas, so whites would not be disturbed.

In the first days, marchers were routinely carried off to jail. That reduced the number of adults willing to take part. Going to jail often meant losing your job.

By May 2, leaders decided that to keep the movement going, they would have to encourage schoolchildren to take part. That day, as hundreds of teenagers filed out of a rally at Sixteenth Street Baptist Church, their sole aim was to march to Birmingham City Hall (in the white part of town) to demonstrate and pray on the steps. Six hundred were arrested.

By the next day, the jails were full. The city's aim henceforth would be to disperse the protesters, without taking them into custody.

As the marchers left the church, again on their way to City Hall, fire hoses went off. Many fled. But, trying to hold their balance against the spray, ten sat down on the sidewalk, encouraging others to remain with them.

Another tactic was needed. The fire department had special high-pressure monitor guns, which shot water from two hoses through one nozzle. They had been advertised as miracles of modern fire fighting, able to strip bark off trees or knock the mortar out of bricks. They were trained on the protesters.

That cut down substantially on the number of hoses available, however, and some of the demonstrators began streaming past policemen toward City Hall. Others started pelting officers with rocks and bottles.

The city then turned loose its K-9 police dog unit. Many were attacked; some were injured badly enough to require hospitalization.

Nobody died. A military strategist might have called it a tactical success. But the photographs of that awful encounter flashed around the world, designating Birmingham as the capital of segregation and awakening millions to the struggle in the South.

One morning this week, I took the new "Freedom Walk" through the park, among the statues designed to make you feel how those marchers felt. A rush of thoughts hit.

About the raw courage of those children. About the thousands of undereducated people who walked off sharecropper farms to struggle out of poverty in Birmingham's steel mills. About how instead of educating them, their state government waved the bloody shirt of racism so the economically powerful could remain politically powerful.

About Molly Ivins's injunction that ignorance is the root of all evil, and nobody knows the truth.

There are sacred places in any city, places like Sloss Furnace where poor men worked themselves to death scratching out a future.

Think of the story of those marchers as you stand in the cool morning air, with the Sixteenth Street Baptist Church behind you and the man coming up behind the statue of Dr. King. Look past the figures on the Freedom Walk toward the higher ground at the center of the park, where a fountain runs water through the gulf that separates us.

You'll understand that place is sacred, too.

RON CASEY

A Divided Alabama Must Have More People for the Middle

August 13, 1993, *Birmingham News*

It was one of those flashbacks that come out of nowhere into the mind's eye.

We were driving down a country road last weekend listening to an Emmylou Harris tape on the way to take my son to summer camp.

There came the faintest memory of myself as a little boy about his age in the back seat of an ancient Chrysler listening to Hank Williams sing "Poor Old Kaw-Liga" about the wooden Indian who never got a kiss.

There was a fog of hazy recall—about men in fedora hats, overalls, and short-sleeve cotton shirts; about women who actually wore aprons.

About the thirty-five years between Hank Williams and Emmylou Harris in Alabama.

A lot has changed. Not all of it good.

While the state expended every waking hour fighting *Brown vs. Board of Education*, schools in other countries were being vastly improved by governments that figured out the United States' economic power was grounded in excellent public education.

While George Wallace warned us about the "Black Bloc Vote," people in Europe were thinking about trading blocs.

So here we are. Alabama no longer competes with Mississippi and Georgia, but with Germany, Japan, and dozens of other countries.

Seventy-six percent of the people in its work force now will still be there in the year 2000.

Fifty-seven percent of them don't have a high school education. And the Southern Regional Education Board says that by the turn of the century, two-thirds of the new jobs that could come here will require college.

Yet even in the face of that kind of challenge we are a state divided.

You'd have to be crazy—or a politician—to say the racial climate hasn't improved here. But race still affects us in ways that are obvious, and ways not so obvious.

In some counties, there hasn't been a school tax increase passed since court-ordered desegregation.

A black elected official told me a disturbing story at the Democratic convention last year: "The party says, 'We've got a candidate coming down through your neck of the woods; how about helping him out?' So you help, thinking you're being a party man, and the party will help you one day. But then, when you tell them you want to run for office yourself, they look at you funny. They ask, 'What does Joe Reed say about it?'"

Some barriers went down. Some new ones went up.

This week, there has been a string of letters from people calling Howell Heflin a traitor for voting against the Daughters of the Confederacy's Stars and Bars insignia. There was another string complaining about the new statue of the police dogs in Kelly Ingram Park and those who "just want to keep things stirred up."

The United Daughters of the Confederacy aren't waving a Confederate battle flag out of a pickup truck. They are ladies who celebrate perhaps an overly romanticized version of the Civil War for the courage and devotion to a noble cause shown in it. But those are the same virtues celebrated by the statue of the police dogs in the park.

Nobody connects the dots.

Race isn't the only thing that separates us, either. When the state legislature starts talking about paying for education reform, the debate quickly deteriorates into class warfare. "It's the big mules trying to trample the little man," you hear from some junior college official who mostly is concerned about whether his own job gets trampled.

"It's just that tax-and-spend crowd throwing money at the problem," you hear from people, many of whom most certainly know that while our schools need a lot of things, one of them is surely more money.

The most damaging division in this state, however, isn't about race, or class, or politics. It is between the people, on one hand, who believe that everything is all right because it's always been that way, and those who believe everything is wrong, because this is, after all, darkest Alabama.

There have to be more people in the middle. People who understand there is as much value in a culture which produces a Hank Williams and an Emmylou Harris—or, for that matter, an Erskine Hawkins and a Lionel Richie—as in any other.

But who also know that some fundamental changes have to be made.

The most important of those is the kind of education we give the majority of our children, the kind of chance they get to compete with other children around the world.

There will be a major effort this fall to give Alabama a first-class school system. We can argue about how that should happen, but we ought to accept from the outset that it has to happen.

And we ought to push for it not as blacks or whites, poor or rich, Republican or Democrat, but as people of Alabama.

Because we owe that to the children in the back seat, and the fading memories in overalls.

BAILEY THOMSON

Clarence Cason's Shade

Alabama Heritage magazine, spring 2001

On his way to Sunday school in Talladega, Alabama, five-year-old Clarence Cason was rolling a nickel on the pavement when a horse and buggy passed him and drew up in front of the sheriff's office. The boy could see feet and legs dangling from the buggy's rear. As Cason recounted more than thirty years later, men on horseback followed closely behind the buggy. Dismounting, they walked into the courthouse, where they summoned several citizens whom the boy knew. The men went out and removed the body of a black man, which lay in the courthouse's corridor until they could locate someone to open a locked door for them.

The boy ran on to church, fearful that he would be late, but he stopped upon realizing he had lost his nickel at the courthouse. He went back and saw that by this time the men had opened the locked door and were lounging in their chairs on the courthouse steps as if nothing unusual had happened. One of them helped young Cason find his nickel, which was intended for the collection plate, and the boy was off again. He slipped quietly into the Sunday school room just as the first song was under way.

"At this moment I cannot recall that I heard anybody, then or later, say anything about the lynching," Cason later wrote. But the experience showed how this peculiar Southern problem ran much deeper in society than sporadic mob violence, even in communities that considered themselves "cultured." Until the best people stepped forward and risked their own personal and commercial standing to denounce the evil practice, it would continue to agitate and disgrace a region that otherwise seemed languorous and dreamy on the surface.

Race, violence, and climatic determinism would figure largely in the adult

Cason's writing about his native South, particularly after he returned to The University of Alabama at age thirty-one to teach journalism. He belonged to that restless generation of Southern intellectuals who, between the world wars, questioned the South's stubborn traditionalism, even as they tried to explain and defend its distinctiveness. From his professorial perch in Tuscaloosa, he penned polished essays for leading national publications, while contributing weekly editorials for newspaper readers. As a journalist in academia, he cultivated a broad audience for his eloquent though tentative observations about the "character" of a region that seemed to be a separate province.

In 1935 Cason collected his thoughts in a book of essays titled *90° in the Shade*. In it, he declared that climate and the relaxation afforded by field and stream had given Southerners excellent reasons for their laziness. Still, he wrote, one could see "there is much work that ought to be done below the Potomac." Above all, blacks continued to be lynched, even in civilized places such as Tuscaloosa, where in 1933 two notorious incidents followed on the heels of the infamous Scottsboro case. Cason's response to such horror, as well as to other endemic problems such as poverty and demagoguery, was to call for "a quiet revolution" in politics and race relations.

Just days before his book's publication, however, Cason killed himself. He left no explanation, but apparently he feared angry reaction from fellow citizens to his mild criticism and gentle suggestions. Many people later would associate Cason's self-destruction with that of another tragic figure from this period, W. J. Cash of North Carolina. Indeed, Cash in his *Mind of the South* shared Cason's fascination with the cotton mill industry and the region's peculiar politics. But Cash's suicide in 1941 following his book's critical success was the result of mental illness and not fear of rejection, as appears to have been the case with the Alabamian.

Cason was born in Ragland, Alabama, on December 20, 1898, and grew up in Talladega, where his father, Eugene P. Cason, was a doctor. From observing his father's practice, the boy learned how difficult life could be for Alabama's poor whites and blacks, many of whom lacked the money to pay for the services. "Experiences of this kind do not constitute scientific data," the son later wrote. "But they clutch the heart."

Cason followed his father to The University of Alabama. Fellow students remembered the slightly built young Cason as a dreamy poet, who favored flashy clothes and answered to the name "Chico." Immersing himself in the literary life of the campus, he joined the Blackfriars Club, where he studied acting with Hudson Strode, who was only a few years older but already had returned to teach at his alma mater. Cason's interests also gravitated to journalism, which he learned by working on student publications and doing stints during the summers for newspapers, including work in Washington, D.C., with the *New York Times*.

Upon graduation in 1917, Cason took a reporting job with the *Birmingham News*. But the Great War soon sucked him and other members of his generation into its conflagration. An enlistee in the U.S. Army, he became an expert in the use of the Vickers machine gun and spent six months in France teaching at an aerial gunnery school. After his discharge in February 1919, Cason worked for a string of newspapers, including the *Louisville Courier-Journal*. He also taught at a high school in Louisville and attended a theological seminary. Still not satisfied, he enrolled at the University of Wisconsin for graduate studies in English literature. He earned a master's degree and worked toward a doctorate, while teaching journalism and literature. In 1925, he moved to the University of Minnesota, where he taught journalism as an assistant professor. Two years later, he married Louise Elliott Rickeman of Galena, Illinois.

During his stay in the North, Cason encountered prejudice toward Southerners, as when one of his deans asked him, "What seems to be the air of scholarship in the South—to sit on the front porch and drink lemonade?" Yet he also was exposed to the ideas of Willard Bleyer, a pioneer at Wisconsin in transforming journalism into an academic discipline. Unlike Bleyer, however, who pursued the history of newspapers and other scholarly contributions, Cason preferred creative work. In his essays and other writings, he combined an intense desire to explain the world with a poetic sensitivity.

In 1928, Dean Charles H. Barnwell at The University of Alabama persuaded Cason to return to the campus and organize a journalism department within the College of Arts and Sciences. The invitation included freedom to pursue whatever model of instruction that Cason deemed appropriate. In that day, most newspapermen learned their craft on the job, as Cason had done. They typically advanced in the newsroom from clerk to cub reporter and then to more demanding tasks as writers and editors. At Alabama, Cason sought to impart his love of the liberal arts to his journalism students, whom he believed in educating rather than merely training for a vocation. He used the Socratic method to elicit thinking, and he did not impose his opinions upon his listeners. He would sit on the side of his desk, pipe in hand, and draw students into a conversation about the week's news or some topic he had assigned. He guided their work with thoughtful criticism. Gould Beech, who edited the student newspaper, the *Crimson White*, and later became an editorial writer and political activist in Alabama, recalled, "He was always encouraging you to learn more, to find out more, not coming to conclusions until you knew all the facts."

Cason quickly enjoyed the esteem of his students and colleagues. One reason was the fact that he continued to work as a journalist himself. His essays appeared in leading journals such as the *Nation, Yale Review, Virginia Quarterly Review, Sewanee Review,* and *Outlook.* His pieces also were published in the *New York Times Magazine,* the *Baltimore Sun,* and other prestigious newspapers. He contributed regularly to the editorial pages of the *Birmingham News,* even doing a summer stint to fill in for a vacationing writer. He was also in demand as a public speaker, and his comments attracted editorial attention. Such prodigious work inspired Grover Hall's *Montgomery Advertiser* to describe Cason as one of the "most brilliant and engaging thinkers in Alabama."

As a writer, Cason leaned toward the progressive Regionalists, who, under the inspiration of Howard W. Odum at the University of North Carolina, advocated planning and other modern methods to address the South's problems. But Cason's criticisms of his region stopped short of ridiculing its customs. For example, he did not join the followers of H. L. Mencken in excoriating the South's churches for their provincialism. Rather, he saw them as helping to hold together their communities, particularly those in isolated rural areas. Likewise, he refrained from condemning racial segregation—a position that would have been a radical step for a Southern liberal. Cason's arguments were carefully nuanced to support what he called "intelligent and conservative" attitudes on both sides of the color line. He condemned lynching and racial demagoguery—those barbaric practices associated with the region's common whites—while encouraging solidarity between blacks and the region's white aristocrats.

Cason also found much to admire in the work of the Agrarians at Vanderbilt, who often were at odds with the Regionalists' emphasis on economic development. In 1931, he wrote Donald Davidson at Vanderbilt that the group's recent book, *I'll Take My Stand,* was an artistic triumph. Nevertheless, Cason deplored how Davidson and his fellow authors had used agrarianism to string together essays that defended Southern tradition. Their method put too much emphasis on making a living. "I wonder whether a somewhat industrialized South will not still retain many of the human traits which we revere as characteristic of our section," Cason wrote.

In 1934 Cason contributed a chapter to *Culture in the South,* published by the University of North Carolina Press and edited by the press's director, W. T. Couch. In the spring of that year, Cason wrote Couch, "I have had this little volume in mind in all the essays I have attempted on Southern subjects during the last six years." The result was to be Cason's *90° in the Shade.* Many of the ideas would be distilled from Cason's previously published essays, but the author also expanded upon his reinterpretations and received many suggestions from Couch. The two men exchanged enthusiastic letters about the project. Yet, as the publication date neared, Cason grew somber and fearful that his criticism of the region, no matter how gently offered, might antagonize his fellow Southerners. "I am convinced that it will be exceedingly difficult for me to remain in Tuscaloosa after the book is published," the author wrote on May 4, 1935.

Earlier that day, he had sent an urgent telegram to Couch, warning that the book's dust jacket drew an unfortunate comparison to Carl Carmer's controversial *Stars Fell on Alabama,* a social commentary on the South that had portrayed The University of Alabama as being little concerned with intellectual life. Couch sought to calm his writer by suggesting he was simply suffering from "extreme nervousness." Cason's book combined good writing with straight thinking, and it would be a success, Couch predicted. "If I were in your place, I would go fishing and forget the whole thing."

About this time, James Saxon Childers, literary editor of the *Birmingham News,* interviewed Cason at the author's home and found him "frightfully worried." Childers sought to assuage his fears by mapping out a campaign to assure a good reception for the book. Following the interview, Childers wrote a favorable article for his Sunday edition and sent a copy for his inspection. The next morning, Childers learned that Cason had shot himself on the previous evening, May 8, in his office at the Journalism Department. Cason's wife found him slumped on a chair, with an automatic pistol nearby.

Speaking for a shocked campus, University of Alabama President George Denny, in his comments to the *Tuscaloosa News,* declared, "[Cason] was one of the finest members of our faculty, a brilliant teacher and leader in his field of work." Meanwhile, Couch informed the *News* that Cason's death was the result of "temporary unbalance caused by worry." The press would have halted publication had its editors known of Cason's mental state.

Later, in a private letter, Couch confided to Jonathan Daniels, editor of the Raleigh *News & Observer,* that Cason had no reason to fear adverse reaction in Tuscaloosa: "I have never read any book about the South that I thought was written with better humor and was less likely to arouse antagonism." The book editor described Cason as a "quiet, gentle, retiring person who abhorred controversy. At the same time he was aware of the need for honest frank discussion." In a letter to Hudson Strode, Couch wrote, "I am afraid I can never forgive [Cason] for wiping out a talent that in my opinion is so rare as to be almost nonexistent."

Cason's fears were not entirely imaginary. The year before his death, a professor from Alabama College at Montevallo had an encounter with Tuscaloosa's Ku Klux Klan, when about forty hooded members searched his car. This incident caused John Temple Graves II to write, "We don't blame Tuscaloosa for being afraid but the thing they have to fear is not Communism. It is Ku Kluxism, lynching Moron-ism." Meanwhile, Merlin N. Hanson claimed he had been

fired from the *Mobile Register* a year earlier for writing in a Philadelphia magazine about people of mixed racial heritage. Cason may have overreacted, Hanson
concluded, but he had written truthfully "about a section that carries its feeling
around on the end of its nose."

Despite such prickly sensitivity to criticism, local reaction to Cason's book
was positive. A reviewer for the *Tuscaloosa News,* who was himself a scion of a
prominent Black Belt family in Greensboro, found nothing offensive. The late
author had drawn his conclusions fairly and did not seek to sensationalize the
South, Hamner Cobbs concluded. "He wrote [his book] as a liberal critic who,
loving the South, nevertheless hoped to contribute in his own modest way to its
progress, who might help in stirring it from its lethargy." Meanwhile, the state's
editorial pages mourned the loss of "Chico," as the writers affectionately called
Cason.

Nationwide, Cason's book inspired reviews and notices in many leading newspapers and periodicals. Daniels observed in the *Saturday Review* that the South
needed more authors who could write so intelligently. A reviewer for the *New
York Times* thought Cason had been too easy on his section's sins, such as lynching and child labor. By contrast, *Time* Magazine's reviewer reported Cason,
having cast "his dissatisfied eye over the Southern scene, finds it on the whole
down-at-the-heel, lazy, complacent, resigned, ignorant, cynical, exasperating."
The reviewer, speculating that fear of local reaction drove Cason to suicide,
wondered, "Had he jeopardized a pleasant life for the doubtful fame of writing
a controversial book?" In response to *Time's* review, one of Cason's former students, Charles Alldredge, wrote the editors, "The University of Alabama is nar-
row, I will admit, but both faculty and students appreciated Cason for what he
was, the ablest of teachers."

What were the ideas that drew such attention to Cason and ultimately led
him to suicide, after he sought to "psychograph" this separate province of the
United States? Two great elements, he wrote, conditioned Southern culture.

The first was climate—specifically the dog days of summer that drove people
to the shade, or better yet, to the fishing holes. Languor disinclined Southerners
to address the problems that plagued their region, such as disease, exhausted agriculture, and ignorance. How different Southerners were in 1935 from, say, residents of Wisconsin, whose unpredictable and severe winters accustomed them
to accept change and new ideas.

Cold weather did not produce the kind of enervating effect upon Northern-
ers that sultry summers inflicted upon Southerners, Cason argued.

The South's second great conditioning element, Cason wrote, was the presence of African Americans. At that time, about one in four Southerners was
black, and the South remained the great center of African American population

in America, although migration was continuing to take blacks out of the region and into Northern cities. Relatively few blacks could vote in Alabama and other Deep South states, having lost the franchise around the turn of the century. Opportunities for education and advancement were pitifully few. Schools for black students typically were inadequate and well below even the modest levels of education afforded whites.

"Quite aside from such abstract concepts as human freedom and justice, can the South longer afford to jeopardize its economic future by continuing to harbor various delusions which are calculated to keep so large a part of its population in poverty and ignorance?" Cason asked. White Southerners, he argued, had to make room for blacks to take their proper place as good citizens and productive workers.

These two elements—a hot climate and a large population of blacks—had made the South a different kind of place, Cason believed. Unfortunately, this separate province had demonstrated complacency and even hostility to progress.

And what were the consequences for failing to think and act in more progressive ways? For one, Cason argued, Alabama and the Deep South in 1935 labored under politics that offered more sport than leadership. Demagogues pitted the poor white against the poor black, thereby helping condemn both to marginal existence. Another consequence involved the South's churches, so powerfully present in every community and too often turned inward rather than addressing the social problems at their doorsteps. Finally, Cason wrote, Alabama in the 1930s was not ready for the next wave of industrialism. It offered cheap and docile labor at a time when America was becoming the technological leader of the world. The South's challenge was not the exploitation of workers in the mills and mines, although such incidences did occur. Rather, the question was "whether the introduction of new machines will not gradually remove the necessity for any kind of unskilled labor—children, women, or men."

Let us now turn the clock forward to our own time. How have Clarence Cason's observations fared? Obviously, Cason underestimated the power of air-conditioning to transform the Deep South. He even sounded silly when he predicted Southerners would reject artificial cooling, preferring to let the summer heat remain a "welcome ally in that it makes the inside of houses and offices agreeably uninviting, if not actually prohibited territory." Once air-conditioning tamed its summers, especially during the booming years after World War II, the South made its sunny climate a great selling point for attracting immigrants and new industries. After all, who cares about one-hundred-degree weather if one feels it only while racing from an air-conditioned Mercedes to a glass, air-conditioned office?

But what about race? Does it not continue to condition Southerners at every level? Yes, it remains a divisive, difficult issue, but hardly one that is confined to the Deep South. Many of the racial problems Alabamians and other Southerners confront today are similar to those of, say, New York, Illinois, or even Wisconsin. Cason probably would be astounded at how racial relations have improved in Alabama. Black citizens now have equal access to public education and other public facilities. They hold legislative, municipal, and county offices. And while acts of racism persist, our black citizens are no longer subjected to systematic terror by hooded murderers and lynch mobs. We know from the hindsight of experience that racial attitudes can be remarkably amenable to positive change, given sufficient determination at the federal level to enforce legal equality.

Cason's generation of liberal Southerners did not have such experience to guide them in assessing white Southerners' attitudes. Instead, they saw what appeared to be an intractable allegiance to white supremacy, as reflected not only in Jim Crow laws and state constitutions but also in the folkways of the region. Under such conditions, they argued that the best solution was to make "separate but equal" true in its full meaning, rather than in terms of segregation alone.

So if climate no longer impedes our progress and race has become less of a Southern issue and more of a national one, what elements condition the Deep South's culture today? Moreover, what deficiencies keep Alabama and some of its neighbors at or near the bottom in comparisons of income, education, and health? The South's distinctiveness continues to be argued in both positive and negative ways even today, just as it was in Cason's time.

One important "conditioning element," to use Cason's term, is the tension between persistent rural values that have been shaped by farm and town for generations and the emerging urbanization that is sprawling along the major interstates. By the end of the 1930s, for example, only about thirty percent of Alabamians lived in urban places. Today sixty-eight percent of the population is in the metropolitan areas. Pine trees now grow on former cotton fields, after farm families departed for urban jobs.

But even with this urbanization, we Alabamians—probably more than most Americans—value our traditions and cling to our old ways of thinking and acting. In some ways, this continuity is our strength. Alabama feels like home to many people who grew up here. We maintain our connections to country churches where our ancestors lie buried. We remain connected to large extended families, though we may not live so close to our relatives as did earlier generations. And many of us prefer to drive pick-ups even when we can afford nice automobiles.

Still, we Alabamians have a nasty habit of ignoring social problems until some outside authority, such as the federal courts, forces us to pay attention. We remain inordinately suspicious of government and prefer that someone else pay for its services. And more recently, we have failed to plan adequately for suburban growth. Within the last generation, Alabamians have failed to reform their antiquated and racist 1901 constitution, as well as their woefully unjust tax system. Yet the need for such reforms grows more intense with each passing year.

Success or failure in resolving this tension between the pull of our rural past and the push for our urban present will determine what Alabama looks like in the year 2035—the one hundredth anniversary of Cason's book. His call for a quiet revolution—one that would inspire a more realistic attitude about our problems and a determination to solve them—echoes through the decades to our own time. As in his day, Alabamians cannot be content to lie in the shade, making excuses for our languor. There is too much work to do.

V

Personal

Infrequently, but to fine effect, Thomson and Casey wrote personal essays. Often these too contained rigorous reporting, or drew on extensive reading. But the "I" is in full force. An exception in the following section is Casey's Christmas column on Jimmy Carter teaching Sunday School in Plains, Georgia. Though "objectively" reported and written, this piece pairs nicely with Thomson's essay on religion, and clearly reflects some of Casey's own ideas about faith and community.

Thomson would say he heard far more from readers about the personal columns than the political ones. No doubt many enjoyed the change of pace, as well as getting to see the humorous and tender sides of writers who so often and so passionately argued for reform.

BAILEY THOMSON

Heirs to Faith

December 25, 1995, *Mobile Press-Register*

I was first exposed to religion while sitting next to my mother on the piano bench as she played hymns at the Methodist Church in Aliceville. I can recall going to Sunday school long before I could read.

Most Alabamians, I suppose, carry similar memories. The faith of their fathers and mothers tugs powerfully upon their souls. Such experiences are part of who they are as well as what they believe.

Robert Drake wrote a poignant short story called "Amazing Grace," which captures the moment in a child's life when he discovers his place among the faithful. A boy wanted to go to the picture show; instead, his parents insisted he go with them to a church dinner on the ground, where a distant female relative with buckteeth and dyed hair pushed her "cormel" cake into his overflowing plate. In the meeting house, however, the sullen child noticed tears in his father's eyes. An epiphany gripped the boy. He knew, without anyone telling him, why his father wept.

In Alabama, as in other parts of our vast Bible-believing region, the dominant faith is born-again Protestantism. Groups such as Catholics and Jews exert influence, too, especially in cities such as Mobile where they have sizable congregations. But conservative Protestants set the tone for life in Alabama. Much of our culture, from politics right down to football, is interpreted through the prism of what is often called the "old time religion." It is difficult to be precise about such things. Among Protestants, faith begins and ends with the individual; so there are almost infinite shades of belief.

Serious differences divide Alabama's conservative Christians. The most bitter fighting afflicts the Southern Baptists, who teeter on the edge of schism within their national convention. So intense is the dispute over biblical "inerrancy" that a group of moderates has formed a separate fellowship.

Outsiders may have difficulty understanding such intense quarrels over whether the Bible must be read literally, right down to the Genesis account of creation. In part, these struggles reflect the monolithic nature of conservative Protestantism in the South.

In the North, by contrast, the conservative Protestantism that prevailed in the nineteenth century gradually eroded from massive immigration of non-Protestants. Moreover, many Northern churches embraced newer forms of theology, which placed less emphasis on emotional conversion.

Not surprisingly, revivalism moved South, much like the textile industry. In this century, the great revivalists have been Southerners such as Billy Graham. Indeed, the Southern Baptists now form the nation's largest Protestant denomination. Worldwide, evangelical and Pentecostal religion often has a Southern flavor.

In Alabama, the "modernism" that preachers rail against has, in fact, made few inroads. A *Mobile Register*/University of South Alabama poll last May found that ninety-five percent of Alabamians believe in a literal hell, compared with about sixty percent of people nationwide. At a time when the cultural and economic ground is shaking under Americans' feet, traditional Protestantism remains a solid rock for most Alabamians, whether they are "bypass Baptists" or members of booming non-denominational churches.

Social critics delight in pointing out that the church hour on Sunday is the most segregated time. That criticism ignores, however, the historic independence of black churches. When slaves won their freedom, they moved quickly to establish their own congregations, independent of white control.

In recent years, whites and blacks in Alabama have made tentative steps toward a common religious ground.

The Rev. Clarence Lett, who is the pastor at Macedonia Baptist in Daphne, said that his congregation embraces the same biblical principles as its white counterpart up the road at Eastern Shore Baptist. They belong to different national conventions, but the two churches are both Southern and Baptist.

On Sunday mornings, worship gets lively at Macedonia, which counts about six hundred members. There are three choirs, and services may go beyond the regular hour and a half.

Macedonia shares with Eastern Shore a willingness to experiment with new forms of music and outreach. The two congregations even meet on the softball diamond, as each strives to supplement religious services with recreational and educational programs.

Lett, who is seventy and near retirement, said he learned early in his ministry about the value of church activity. An old preacher advised him, "Keep the people working, or they'll start working on you."

Grant Barber, who is the pastor at fast-growing Eastern Shore Baptist, keeps his flock working, too, often ministering to people who are not even members of the church. They attend various sessions during the week to help them cope with personal crises. Other people come looking for a spiritual home, although they may have no background in Baptist beliefs.

On a recent Sunday morning, the service was relaxed and warm, with no "high church" trappings, such as liturgical readings or even choir robes. The congregation heard two soloists sing contemporary Christian music, with taped backgrounds. Barber began by telling a joke on himself, putting listeners into a comfortable frame of mind to hear his message.

"We can't structure things the way we used to," Barber said later in his small, modestly furnished office. "We want to do something to reach the community."

While evangelism remains the main emphasis among Southern Protestants, there has also been an often understated concern for improving social conditions. Wayne Flynt, who is both an ordained Southern Baptist minister and a distinguished history professor at Auburn University, frequently calls upon fellow believers to honor their convention's long-standing commitment to social justice. Earlier Alabama Baptist leaders opposed child labor, the notorious convict lease system, substandard housing, and other societal ills.

In a case study of Birmingham, Flynt found that church rolls actually grew fastest when many of the city's Baptist leaders openly embraced what is known as the Social Gospel during the first decades of this century. This activist approach taught that Christians had an obligation to improve society as well as to save souls. Leaders such as L. L. Gwaltney, the influential editor of the *Alabama Baptist,* saw no conflict between social concerns and salvation, considering them as complementary parts of the total Gospel.

The Woman's Missionary Union, based in Birmingham, is the largest female Christian organization in the United States. Through its auspices, Alabama Baptist churches this year gathered canned goods and money to feed hungry people. Next year, the WMU will focus on racial reconciliation to combat racism.

Dellanna O'Brien, who directs the WMU, said Southern Baptists give generously to mission causes, but she is not satisfied that they are reaching out enough to their communities. "In a state with such a large Baptist membership, we find some of the deepest pockets of poverty," Ms. O'Brien said. "Yet, we seldom address the issue of getting at the root causes."

Meanwhile, Alabama's United Methodists, who belong to the nation's second largest Protestant denomination, have been more openly supportive of social causes and less plagued by theological squabbles. In part, this difference reflects the Methodists' centralized government, as opposed to the Baptist belief in congregational control. Since the Southern and Northern Methodist branches reunited in 1939, a national agenda has predominated, often to the dismay of conservative Southern Methodists.

Like the Presbyterians, Alabama's United Methodists are more reserved in their worship. Those of us who grew up in these traditions often feel uncomfortable around emotional conversions, although they are not unknown, particularly at revival time. An evangelizing fervor helped spread Methodism along the Alabama frontier in the early 1800s. Many churches continue to emphasize the "warm feeling" that their founder John Wesley and his circuit-riding successors infused into followers.

At Trinity United Methodist in the tiny Weoka community in Elmore County, the Rev. Michael White said "the Lord is moving" among the church's 107 members. Nine people joined this year. Many members are baby boomers, who want their children to grow up with church experiences.

White, who is thirty-four, said most Methodists in Alabama are conservative and adhere closely to Scriptural authority, although they do not insist upon reading the Bible literally. "At Trinity, we're all Bible-believing Christians," White said. "We take John Wesley's words to heart about being a people of one book." White's own biblical study has convinced him that the world's end is near. "It does appear that God is preparing to draw things to a close."

To hasten the return of more lost sheep while time remains, White has taught himself how to publish over the Internet. His church maintains a Web page, and he produces another one for his United Methodist conference. In his view, such efforts are a modern equivalent to the old camp meetings that Alabama Methodists once staged to convert sinners and reinforce the faithful. As communication has changed, so has the church's methods of evangelizing.

No Christians have understood better the possibilities of modern communication than have the Pentecostals, who have been tireless revivalists. Today, they are the world's most dynamic Protestant group, attracting millions of enthusiasts from outside the United States, particularly in poorer areas such as Latin America.

Pentecostals continue an emotional style of religion that broke out almost spontaneously across the Southern frontier, beginning in 1801. People found Christ and shouted and jumped with joy, sometimes falling to the ground in ecstasy. Gradually, what became the mainline Southern churches achieved a middle-class respectability and grew more restrained in their worship. Even among the Baptists and Methodists, a kind of starched-shirt decorum displaced the earlier spontaneity.

Into this void stepped first the Holiness and later the Pentecostal movements, appealing to the state's dispossessed people. In fact, Alabama became a staging ground for the Assemblies of God, which organized in 1914. Like most other Protestant branches, these new churches read their Bibles literally, while predicting the imminent return of Christ. The Pentecostals looked to the early church. They even claimed that God had restored in them spiritual gifts such as speaking in tongues and faith healing.

Critics dismissed these congregations as "holy rollers." In fact, mainline churches paid little attention until after World War II, when the Pentecostals burst onto the revival scene with ministers such as Oral Roberts who could pack thousands of believers into their tents. The simple message of salvation appealed to followers, as did the spirited music. With this formula, the Pentecostals turned informal worship into entertainment, which fit well into cable television's insatiable appetite for programming.

David E. Harrell, a historian at Auburn University, has studied this phenomenon. He predicts that half the world's Christians will be Pentecostal or at least tongues-speaking by the year 2000. "They have become the cutting edge of missionary activity all over the world," he said.

At the turn of the century, an Englishman named Sir William Archer toured the former Confederacy and declared that the South was "the most simply and sincerely religious country that I ever was in." It was not "priest-ridden" like Ireland or steeped in theology like Scotland. "But it is a country in which religion is a very large factor in life, and God is very real and personal."

Since Archer's visit, Alabama and other Southern states have come to resemble the rest of the nation with their sprawling suburbs and industries. Even the South's television announcers speak the same "network English." But one distinctive Southern quality endures, and that is the region's great affinity for old time religion. It has taken new forms and even further divided along theological fault lines, but the essential faith remains.

I began this essay with a personal note, and I shall end it with one. My people came to this country as Scotch-Irish Presbyterians. They are buried in church yards along the way in Virginia, South Carolina, and Alabama. They became Methodists only in my father's generation, when his mother converted the family. My father seldom went to church. "Just the same old crowd there every Sunday," he used to say. Instructing the children in the faith fell to my mother, and she had us in church every Sunday. Thus, there is an unbroken tradition from my generation as far back as I can know.

My daughter is only eleven, but she already knows a great deal about her ancestral faith. She attends church regularly. As we were driving to the airport last week to pick up her grandmother, I asked her what she would probably remember most from this experience. She thought a while and then replied, "Mama's singing."

I don't think she saw my tears.

RON CASEY

Carter Quietly Shares Christmas Message

December 25, 1998, *Birmingham News*

Drive past the giant, grinning peanut for a couple hundred yards of rural land-scape. The small, brick church is on the right, in the grove next to a cotton field.

Inside, an older gentleman is standing below the wide, low roof arches that look like wings, talking about the history of the community.

Then without fanfare or warning, the thirty-ninth president of the United States walks out of a back room in his blazer, gray slacks, and striped shirt with no tie, and sits on the front pew, waiting for the historian to finish.

On the Sunday after the House of Representatives has impeached President Clinton, and American warplanes have devastated military targets in Iraq, Jimmy Carter is about to teach his Sunday school lesson at the Plains, Georgia, Mara-natha Baptist Church.

"Are there any visitors here?" he asks. He knows full well there are. The sanc-tuary is almost full, and the church has only 128 members. More than seven thou-sand people came to his Sunday school classes last year. On one day, eighteen foreign countries were represented.

Rosalynn Carter walks in shortly after her husband began to speak and takes a seat on the front pew. During his talk, he will often refer to her: "Rose, what was the name of that guy?" "When did we go there?"

He begins each lesson with a brief comment on the news. Part of the news is that daughter Amy is pregnant, but they don't know what sex the child will be. "Jimmy," Rosalynn interjects. "She said it was no bigger than a butter bean. How could she know?"

He finds what has happened in Iraq senseless, he says, because there is no long-term plan. And what is happening in Washington he and his good friend Gerald Ford think is deplorable.

His final commentary on those matters will be his Sunday school lesson. It is from Matthew 1:8–21.

It is the story of how Joseph, a simple man, an illiterate carpenter, perhaps, learned that the woman he was engaged to, Mary, was pregnant. "Back when Jesus was about the size of a butter bean," he nods in his wife's direction.

The whole community knew of Mary's pregnancy because in those days women had to go through a cleansing ceremony following their menstrual cycle before they could return to the temple.

Joseph knew that it was not his baby. And he knew that everyone else knew.

A strict interpretation of the law called for one of two punishments for a woman pregnant out of wedlock: she could be stoned to death, or the priests could call down a curse that she never be allowed to bear children again.

But Joseph was a righteous man, the Bible says. "It doesn't say he was a self-righteous man," Carter adds. He knew how to balance the law with grace. He was not willing to have her publicly punished. He showed a compassion, love, and humility that went beyond him; that foreshadowed the teachings of the son Mary would bear.

Only after he had granted his forgiveness did an angel appear to Joseph to reveal that Mary's baby had been placed in her womb by the Holy Spirit.

God made a revelation to Joseph, and he still makes revelations to us every day, the former president says in his quiet monotone. Every time you walk past a homeless person sleeping on a bench under a newspaper, or see someone who is needy or lonely—even though they may not look physically attractive or well-dressed—God is revealing an opportunity for you to act on His behalf.

It's curious, says Carter. As a governor of Georgia, he and the other Southern governors used to have an informal competition to see who could have the least number of prisoners in their penitentiaries; who could come up with the rehabilitation program to keep the largest number out. In those days, if he had ever run a negative ad against an opponent in Georgia, he would have been ruined politically.

Now the competition is to see how many prisoners can get a life sentence, through tough, three-strikes-and-you're-out sentencing laws; to see how many can get the death penalty. Texas kills an average of one convict a week. "If Jesus were here today, I don't think He would be in favor of the death penalty, do you?" he says as the crowd nods. "But then I don't think He would be in favor of abortion either, except to save a mother's life."

On top of harsh laws, contentious, vicious politics floods the nightly news. Popular wars flare up.

Why is it all happening?

Who is to blame?

He pauses for a moment, as though his answer may not go down easily with the audience.

"We are."

Because our officials do not air negative ads without polling first. They would not push the death penalty if people were against it.

"We separate what we can do in our churches from what we do in our public lives and in our business lives," he says. "We can't keep doing that. The balm for America's wounds is to find the grace, charity, love, forgiveness, and humility that Joseph found before that first Christmas."

Then the man whose favorite charity, Habitat for Humanity, will soon build its 100,000th home for the poor, whose Carter Center in Atlanta has interceded in more conflicts than any institution in the world, and whose efforts in poor countries have saved millions from disease and starvation, picks up the small podium he has been using and carries it up the steps of the pulpit platform, placing it in front of the loft for the choir director's use.

He smiles, thanks everyone for coming, and turns to walk back into the background.

RON CASEY

The Thrill of Winning the Pulitzer Is All of Ours to Share

April 12, 1991, *Birmingham News*

Did you ever feel like a brown shoe in a world of tuxedos?

I'm sitting here, the day after the Pulitzer Prize announcements, trying to write a column. But the phone keeps ringing every thirty seconds with another nice person who just wants to issue congratulations.

Those calls make you feel great, and not just because most of them are from people you like and admire. There is a hint of something other than just congratulations in a lot of their voices.

A lot of them are from old newspaper colleagues, government officials, and long lost friends.

But many also are from just everyday newspaper readers, many of whom sound about as excited as you feel.

They are Alabamians.

They are people genuinely proud that their hometown newspaper has won such an award. Their voices, and their sincerity, make you feel wonderful, and very small, at the same time.

On the day after you and your buddies have won a Pulitzer Prize, you can't really concentrate on anything, to be honest about it. You just watch bits and snatches of impressions float by.

Let me tell somebody quick who really deserves this thing or they're sure to take it back.

Wayne Flynt, Bill Barnard, Virginia Van der Veer Hamilton, C. Vann Woodward, and Mills Thornton all should be given a portion of this thing.

All are historians who have done much more in-depth research into the problems and miseries of the South than any editorial page series ever could.

Flynt, especially, deserves a sustained round of applause from everyone in this state.

His book *Poor but Proud: Alabama's Poor Whites* is an inspirational documentary of the rough-cut beauty of many of our ancestors. It ought to be mandatory reading in any history course in this state, along with *Parting the Waters,* Taylor Branch's history of the civil rights movement.

Keith Ward, at the Auburn University Center for Governmental Services, owns a piece also. This guy knows Alabama's tax system like the rest of us know our backyards. And he's not been afraid to tell the truth about its problems, even when he knew that would not be the most expedient thing to do.

Albert Brewer and the Public Affairs Research Council of Alabama at Samford University own part for excellent research.

Joyce Bigbee at the Legislative Fiscal Office has claim on another hunk. You can call that lady with the most esoteric question imaginable about Alabama's financial affairs and within five minutes you'll get a straight answer. She's nice about it, too.

Joey Kennedy and Harold Jackson, editorial writers here, already have a chunk of it. But folks ought to know more what they did to get it.

There were about three months in there when they did the work they normally do every day to put out an editorial page, and then worked on tax reform research and interviews, often on their own time.

A lot of weekend work went into the series which won.

James E. Jacobson, Clarke Stallworth, and Tom Scarritt went over the package of editorials behind us and made it better. The Hanson family published it, with hardly a question. I don't think there are many papers in this state where that would have happened.

Best feeling of the day:

A tie between:

(1) Putting *Editor and Publisher* and the *New York Times* on hold so you can tell your wife you've won a Pulitzer Prize, and:

(2) Getting home to have your three-year-old daughter meet you at the front door, give you a hug, and say, "Daddy, I am glad you won the race."

Most humbling aspect of the thing:

Seeing reporters out in the newsroom popping champagne corks like there was no tomorrow. Most of them are people who put a lot of heart and a lot of hard work into what they do, and they don't get enough for it in return.

The chemistry out in that newsroom was something I'll never forget. It was like one big family had won the *Reader's Digest* Sweepstakes.

No one person was celebrating any harder than another.

Favorite quote:

From reporter Tom Gordon, who put his arm over my shoulder while the champagne party was under way and quietly said, "Wherever your daddy is, you know he's proud."

My daddy died seven years ago.

RON CASEY

Deadlines, Exams, and Lessons in Politics

October 31, 1993, *Birmingham News*

As do all the fortyish, potbellied types who have noticed the tell-tale signs of ac-
cumulated brain cell death in recent years, I like to think my college days were
just yesterday. But I came across a reminder they weren't recently in a book about
Southern politics. It was copy from an ad that ran in the George Wallace–Albert
Brewer governor's race of 1970, my freshman year at The University of Alabama:

IF YOU WANT TO SAVE *Alabama as we know Alabama Remember! The bloc*
vote (Negroes and their white friends) nearly nominated Gov. Brewer on May 5th.
This Black and White Social-Political Alliance MUST NOT DOMINATE THE
PEOPLE OF ALABAMA The spotted alliance must be defeated! This may be your
last chance VOTE RIGHT _ VOTE WALLACE

I'd like to be able to say I was outraged by the overt racism in that ad and
did what I could to prevent an injustice. The truth is that I recall Otis Redding,
football games, and a roommate who knew how to make "Purple Passion" cock-
tails more vividly than that governor's race.

Which is why the three years I was involved with the *Crimson-White* were so
important for me. Nationally, there has been a lot of press in the past few years
about the so-called "Machine," a fraternity coalition which ran campus politics
at the university for decades. This weekend, a large number of people got together in Tuscaloosa to celebrate the one hundredth birthday of its nemesis, the
student newspaper.

The roll-call of state politicians who got their training in the "Machine" is
impressive—from Lister Hill to Bill Baxley. But the list of writers who got some
of their training in the bloodshot, early morning hours of *Crimson-White* publication eves is just as interesting: Nationally known novelists Gay Talese, Mark

Childress, Ann Waldron, and Robert R. McCammon, to name a few. A couple of Pulitzer Prize winners, like Hazel Brannon Smith in 1960s Mississippi. Newspaper people from here to Chicago, to Oakland, to New York, like James E. Jacobson, the editor of this newspaper, or Bailey Thomson, associate editor of the *Mobile Register,* or scores of others.

There is an unspoken bond that usually comes through when you talk to *C-W* people. It's more than just having the same frame of reference of a sometimes grungy old office. It's as if you've all been through the same initiation into professional writing, and even adulthood.

My years at the *Crimson-White* lured me off the sidelines and into a new kind of understanding about community, about the human side of government and the possibilities waiting there. I suspect it has done that for hundreds of students. My father didn't cast a vote until the Supreme Court struck down Alabama's poll tax. He talked politics all the time, but it was always a distant thing, like you would talk about a ballgame or the weather. Government was a them, not a we.

The *C-W* made me understand that government can be changed for better or for worse; that it is something controlled by human people. I recall trying to interview John Sparkman in the college coffeeshop and how adept he was at avoiding even the appearance of a straight answer. He was very bright and intimidating; the first big-time politician I ever questioned as a reporter. About halfway through the interview, he dropped his coffee spoon on the floor. It was as though a bell had rung. This guy's just a person after all.

So many people I first met while working for the *Crimson-White* I have come across again in Alabama politics: Don Siegelman, Marsha Folsom, Jim Zeigler. Roger Lee, who was president of the SGA when I was editor, was a lieutenant for Paul Hubbert three years ago. Steve Windom, who regularly gave me hell about the newspaper's spending habits when he was in the SGA, is a state senator from Mobile. Maybe I feel so much more strongly the irritation at the old Wallace ad now because in the past few years, I have come to know Albert Brewer well enough to call him for advice occasionally. I know what a thoroughly decent, intelligent man he is and how much pain Alabama might have avoided had it not worried so much about "the bloc vote."

The one hundredth anniversary of the *Crimson-White* strikes me on two levels. First are the memories of all-nighters in the middle of a strange curved desk with glue pots everywhere and intermingled anxieties about the stupidity of the SGA budget and the 8 a.m. political science class looming. It was a coming of awareness. And it occurred for me personally as the state itself was in a growing stage.

One hundred years ago, Alabama was only a few years away from adopting a constitution that would ultimately disfranchise two-thirds of those eligible to vote. Most of those politically disinherited were blacks and poor whites. Their exclusion from their own state's government ended only three decades ago with the upheaval of the voting rights movement. Since, it has been a long, slow walk away from the politics of prejudice toward the day when the people of Alabama will run the state of Alabama.

Auburn's Wayne Flynt put it well in a column he wrote for the *News* not too long ago: "Two powerful, complementary patterns are coursing through the veins of Alabamians. They have correctly concluded their leaders have failed them. They are slowly awakening to the awful price we have paid for this failure. And in communities across this state they are coming together to argue, debate, reach consensus, mobilize and demand action."

At a time when the people of Alabama are beginning to crowd the portals of democracy, it's appropriate to celebrate the centennial of an institution like the *Crimson-White,* which over the years brought so many into the arena.

BAILEY THOMSON

Hope Chest

Fall 1998, *Alabama Heritage* magazine

My wife had news when I called her from the Best Western in Monroeville, Alabama. I was attending a literary conference, where writers pondered, among other things, how being Southern had shaped who they were and what they wrote. Such ruminative gatherings are a minor industry for our region, and the local community college was eager to capitalize on Monroeville's claim to Harper Lee and other notable writers.

"We've got the chest," my wife said. "Aunt Zelda had it for us when Sarah and I went by to see her."

The chest? It's at our house?

"I couldn't believe it," my wife said, "but Aunt Mamie told Aunt Zelda it was time to pass the chest down, and we brought it home with us. I was scared to death something would happen to it on the way."

My wife paused. "They gave it to Sarah. Aunt Mamie wanted Sarah to have it."

Sarah is our fourteen-year-old. Many times, I had told her how my grandmother kept the chest on a bureau in her guest bedroom like some museum piece. When I was small, she would allow me to look at the heirloom, but I could never touch it. The leather was cracked and peeling from the studs that bound it to a wooden frame. The ancient lock no longer worked.

The chest, which looks like a miniature foot locker, may have come with my grandmother's people from the British Isles. It was just large enough to hold valuables, such as any jewelry or gold they might have acquired. What turned the chest into a relic, however, was an event that occurred around April 10, 1865. Thereafter, the chest would hold memories, rather than things.

About a week before that date, a detachment of some 1,500 Union cavalry under Brig. Gen. John Thomas Croxton swept into Tuscaloosa County. They fought off Rebel skirmishers around Vance and then occupied Northport and Tuscaloosa, where they burned The University of Alabama. The Bluecoats next attempted to march southwestwardly through Greene and Pickens counties. They hoped to rejoin the main body of federal raiders under the command of Gen. James Harrison Wilson. But Croxton's men, thereafter known as the "lost brigade," became discouraged as they meandered across hostile country. Some of them drowned in swollen rivers. A few fell captive to Southern sympathizers.

Having learned that a brigade of tough Confederates under Wirt Adams was marching toward them from Pickensville, Croxton ordered his men back toward Tuscaloosa. As rain pelted the retreating federals, Adams's men fell on the Union rear, harassing the exhausted Kentuckians. A running fight occurred for some thirty miles, costing the federals about three dozen men, until finally the raiders stumbled into Northport, just across the Warrior River from Tuscaloosa.

Though safe for the moment, Croxton had to keep moving. In addition to a tired brigade, he had as many as two thousand horses and mules that needed forage. With no word of Wilson's whereabouts, he decided this time to march north toward Jasper, taking the old Byler Road. From Jasper, he would march east to find Wilson.

About twelve miles out of Northport, Croxton ordered his men to make camp for a few days near the plantation of John Prewitt, one of the county's wealthiest slaveholders. This respite would allow foraging patrols to strip the country of anything edible.

Mary Ann Kemp's three hundred acres of rolling farmland and woods lay about ten miles away, as the crow flies. Like most of the South's "plain folk," she and her family subsisted on what they grew, selling the surplus to acquire a little cash. They lived in a modest wooden house and stored their corn in a crib nearby.

It's unclear who first saw the Yankees riding up to the home place. The sun was setting, and family members were probably on the front porch, having finished supper. Mary Ann, a widow, was alone with her two grown daughters, Martha and Sarah, and her twelve-year-old son, Robert. Her two oldest sons were away fighting for the Confederacy.

Although word had gone throughout the county that the Yankees were moving northward, Mary Ann probably hadn't expected them to show up so far from the main road. But she thought quickly, as women have always had to do when confronted by menacing men. As the invaders milled around in her yard, she tucked the little chest under her apron and strode out the back door of her house.

She headed for her chicken coop, a primitive structure about three feet long and two feet high. Made of wooden slats, the coop resembled the roof of a house. Farmers used such shelters to protect their chickens at night from predators. They would lift the coop and attract the biddies under it with a tin plate of cracked corn.

Mary Ann raised one end of the coop in the semi-darkness and quickly shoved in the chest where the chicks normally slept.

"What are you doing?" yelled one of the Yankee soldiers.

"I'm just checking on my biddies," she replied. "They're all we're going to have for eating this spring."

"You get back in that house and stay there," the soldier ordered.

Inside the chest was the family's small fortune: $300 in gold that somehow Mary Ann had managed to save. The soldier never came over to investigate, and she returned to the house.

The Yankees commandeered the family's mules and tow wagons and loaded them with the corn they found in the crib. They chased down the chickens in the yard, tied their legs, and threw them on top of the corn. Then they searched the house, but they did not harm the family members.

Finally, they set fire to the crib and rounded up the family's milk cow and calves. Driving the livestock before them, the soldiers left with the wagons and their plunder—but not with the little chest and its treasure. It remained safely hidden under the chicken coop. Because of Mary Ann's quick thinking, there would be money to see the family through the hard year ahead.

I must digress to explain how the little chest came down through the family. Mary Ann's daughter, whom the family called Aunt Sis, never married. When she was seventy, she moved to Berry to live with one of Robert's children, Patience Kemp Kimbrell, who was my grandmother. In the wagon ride to her new home, Aunt Sis brought with her a trunk filled with her clothes. She also brought the little chest, which she kept in her bedroom. Often she told about the marauding Yankees and how her mother had hidden the chest under the chicken coop.

After Aunt Sis died, my grandmother kept the chest. Later, she brought it with her when she and my grandfather moved to Fayette, where they lived in a cottage that always seemed filled with light and laughter. When I visited my grandparents, I would ask to see the chest and look at the old pictures in the bureau's bottom drawer. One of the photographs showed my grandmother and her brothers and sisters in 1903 standing in front of what may have been the original Kemp house. In the photograph, Aunt Sis is seated with the children.

Upon my grandmother's death, the chest passed to Aunt Mamie, the youngest of her six children. Although she has lost much of her eyesight, she directed me recently to the old Kemp homestead, hidden in the brambles and the pines. Near the site, however, and along what is still called "the Kemp Road" in north Tuscaloosa County, remains a tiny cemetery, protected by a chain-link fence.

Here lies buried Mary Ann Kemp, my great-great-grandmother, and next to her, Aunt Sis.

Aunt Mamie is the one who insisted that the chest go not to me, but instead to my daughter, Sarah. Aunt Zelda seemed bemused by that request, but I understood the sentiment. The legacy of their mother's people was that of strong women who persevered in a region that had known a tragically different history from the victorious American version. They were among the conquered people; yet they endured and clung fiercely to their heritage, just as Aunt Sis had protected her little chest during the wagon trip to Berry.

When my wife finished telling me the news about the heirloom, I hung up the telephone and felt an itch to write. Was I responding as a Southerner to my region's peculiar culture, as someone at the literary conference might have suggested? Or was I simply acting upon a universal impulse to understand the human experience through the means of a good story?

I don't know. A more pressing matter was to write these words so that my daughter might store them in the old chest—where they will be safe for the next generation.

RON CASEY

Events for Boomers Get Blurred

July 23, 1999, *Birmingham News*

Two of the most vivid images I am supposed to recall as an official baby boomer (DOB 8/21/51) aren't vivid.

I have an impression of guilt while watching little John-John Kennedy salute his father's casket—guilt because JFK in 1963 was not the most popular politician among middle-income, twelve-year-old, white Alabamians. Watching his son drove home the point that he wasn't just a politician, but a father.

I remember the chill in my spine and the warm, moist air flowing through the den after we cut the window unit off, as my father often did on summer nights, while our family watched a man land on the moon.

The precise details of both have since been erased to make room for college, marriage, and an onslaught of soccer games, dance recitals, dress shirts, and ties.

Yet what I can't seem to remember, America can't seem to forget. Earlier this year, Americans went crazy over John Glenn's return to space. There was a TV miniseries called *The '60s.* Now there is the commemoration of the moon landing and the tragic death of John Kennedy Jr. (I don't know how the Kennedy family survives these things.)

Does our preoccupation with the 1960s come because the biggest segment of the population is the boomers, whose lopsided demographics have always contorted fads, advertising, and news in their direction? Or was there really a special moment that produced more than its supply of heroes?

Both are true.

The 1960s saw television coming into virtually every home. Not the television we have now, with one hundred channels. But network TV, three channels that offered virtually the same news broadcast, with the same slant, every night.

Three networks brought people together rather than blinding them with the light of an information revolution. It made them see for the first time, together, things they had never seen before: Vietnam. The inhumanity of Southern segregation. The courage of a Martin Luther King Jr. All that built a national consciousness.

In the 1960s, most people could easily recall World War II. That made the nation feel invincible. When John Kennedy promised to put a man on the moon within a decade, people believed we could do it, because Americans could do anything. They had never heard of Mai Lai or Watergate.

And in those days, neither was there a huge grazing herd of lobbyists to chew the cud on every detail of Kennedy's proposal for how it might affect the budget and their clients—asking not what they could do for their country, but what their country could kick in for them.

America has become much more corporatized, and so has its government. Instead of being challenged to build a nation of highways, whip the communists, or wage a war on poverty, our highest aspirations are to tweak the HMO system or give somebody a tax advantage. As William Greider wrote last year, in what is a classic description of our change of outlook: what used to be an "underdeveloped country" is now an "emerging market."

And all of this balled up together has ushered in a new age of tackiness—due in no small part to the tabloiding of what once was called the legitimate press and the explosion of new information sources who seem to think that sleazier is always better.

Used to be, if a politician did something in his private life that affected his public life, he was fair game. Otherwise, no.

Now, anything is game. And this symbiotic relationship has developed which makes me want to gag. Newspapers don't report a juicy story because they don't have enough facts or it's not relevant. But a grungy Internet site does report it—which then gives the other media the excuse to report on the Internet report.

If Kennedy promised to put a man on the moon today, doubtless we'd hear a lot of commentary about how it was all just to divert America's attention from Marilyngate, or we'd see reams on how much money was thrown into his presidential campaign by the aerodynamics industry.

You can't go back. The only way to get back to the heroic 1960s is to take away the vast array of information at our fingertips. To make people seem larger than life by massaging the truth about their lives. That is tantamount to saying we'd rather remain huddled in a cave than try to make fire.

And frankly I wouldn't want to go back. Let's not forget that if you were poor in the 1960s you were flat out of luck. If you were black you weren't a citizen here. And schoolchildren regularly endured the anxiety of going to fallout shelters for practice in case of a nuclear holocaust.

Besides, despite all the problems with the 1990s, there is a great hope for something better. I am always impressed with how many of the children you talk to today—children who have never even heard of S&H Green Stamps—have their heads on exactly straight. They're getting better educations than we ever got. They seem more compassionate, more committed to a sense of community.

They'll find a way through. And then someday, after an onslaught of college, marriage, soccer games, and dance recitals, they'll have a hard time remembering the vivid details of Mark McGwire's home run year.

BAILEY THOMSON

Intimations of Mortality

July 7, 1996, *Mobile Press-Register*

"The Child is the father of the Man…"

—William Wordsworth

FRANCONIA—I have a historian friend who is an authority on cemeteries. He studies them as closely as a scholar might pore over ancient texts, seeking internal clues to the dead past. My friend knows just about every burial yard within a 15-county radius of Tuscaloosa—and then some.

In my middle age, I've come to appreciate cemeteries, too. Yes, they tell a lot about who we are and how we got here. But my interest is more personal. As I grow older, I seem to know more people who occupy these hallowed places. I even catch myself silently talking to them when I visit.

It didn't used to be that way. About once a month when I was a boy, our neighbor Miss Winnie would enlist me to drive with her to the cemetery in this ghostly community on the outskirts of Aliceville. She would tend to the graves of her husband and her son, who died before the war while flying a mission from an Army airfield in Montgomery. His airplane crashed just south of our town.

While Miss Winnie weeded, I would wander over to the weathered tombstones that stood like sentinels in the hot sun. Beloved wives, venerated husbands, cherished infants lay, row after row, before me. But to a curious boy, they represented only faded names chiseled into marble.

What a difference 30 or more years can make in one's perception of mortality. I return to this place a middle-aged man, ostensibly to visit the graves of my father and older brother. Something else, however, tugs me along, as I park the car in the late afternoon shade and walk through the gate.

There is no fence to keep anyone out – only an entrance to invite you in. I am the only living soul within sight, and before me spreads the history of my birthplace as if I had opened a book in which graves, rather than chapters, tell the story. The difference now, of course, is that I know so many of the people who have come to rest here since I left home to pursue my own life's journey.

Neither my father nor my brother was born in this area, as were most of the graveyard's occupants. My father moved the family here after the war, when prospects for large-scale farming improved and good land was available. Their permanent rest in this cemetery assures that our family's presence, which ended soon after my departure for college, will have a permanent commemoration. Someone will always say, "Oh yes, the Thomsons. They used to live here. Big family. Farmers. You remember."

Just across from our plot lies that of another family that also is drifting into the mists of the community's collective memory. I knew the two children who now lie next to their parents. I remember how they shared the same big smile and apparently a hereditary cancer, as well.

Near them lies one of the town's finest athletes. Like his father, who is next to him, he died young of a heart attack. In fact, they bore him fatally stricken from the playing field, to the horror of the game's onlookers.

I continue to walk across the green grounds, stopping at familiar names. "When did he die?" I ask myself. Or, "I knew her so well."

One of my favorite teachers lies here. I can hear her through the stillness, exhorting us to be good citizens and keep up with the world's events. "Yes, ma'am, we'll do that. And by the way, did you see that story I wrote the other day? You would have liked it."

Over there lies my old Sunday school teacher. I had forgotten he was here. His lessons could be tedious, but he taught best by example. No church project ever went forward without his name on the list.

Inexorably, I'm pulled to Miss Winnie's grave—her pink marble tombstone identical to that of her husband, a doctor who died a few months after I was born. I pause under the old oak that used to shade us while Miss Winnie did her cemetery chores.

"Will you forgive me," I ask, "that I didn't write up your memories as you wanted me to? I just got too busy with my first newspaper job, and before I knew it you were gone."

As I walk on, I marvel at how every grave contributes to the story, even as the years sometimes shroud the details.

Take the fellow lying over there, next to his mama and daddy. When I was about twelve, he came home with an addiction at a time when such conditions were only whispered about. Few people even saw him as he puttered around his family's place. He once let me visit a small room he had built with scrap lumber.

He had covered the walls with maps, perhaps to remind him of the world he had shut out. Only now, looking at his tombstone, do I realize that he died in his forties, around my own age.

The sun is dipping into the trees across from newly mowed vacant land beyond the last graves. There is ample room for expansion, as our town's living population continues to decline. Maybe they'll all end up here eventually, and their shared history will be complete. Indeed, my historian friend knows of entire communities that have vanished, except for the graveyards where their former occupants peacefully slumber. He even prefers those kinds of cemeteries, because there's a neatness that only the finality of death can provide.

I pause once more at our family's plot before I leave. Four places remain. For the first time in my life, I think about my own last resting place.

RON CASEY

Their Arc in Time Is Passing

July 15, 1994, *Birmingham News*

When my wife was pregnant, the booklet from St. Vincent's said we should pack quarters for the pay phone in her rush-to-the-hospital bag so we could get word out to friends. I think that's why I automatically walked toward the big coin jar in our bedroom when the nurse at Baptist Princeton hung up Wednesday night a week ago.

She said she was calling for Mrs. Ruby Lois Casey; that I should come to the hospital immediately. But I knew she was really saying my mother had died.

My family and I spent the long Fourth of July weekend on the sixth floor of the hospital watching her slip away—or sitting in the waiting area down the hall because we couldn't watch anymore.

Hers was a much more exhausting passage than my father's ten years ago. He went to sleep and didn't wake up. She went to sleep for days, lying almost comatose while struggling for breath as her heart wore out.

Both were from a different Alabama than this one. His name was J. B. That's all. Just J. B. He was from somewhere between Lineville and Ashland in Clay County, though we never found the exact spot where the shack stood.

As a boy, he worked in the fields and helped his grandfather sell Sacred Harp songbooks. He was the singer/demonstrator. (It must have been a real show, because he couldn't carry a tune in a bucket.)

Around the time the Great Depression squashed the South, typhoid fever waylaid his father. He quit school in the tenth grade and later went to work at Woodward Iron Company for a few pennies a day, picking up pieces of coal off the railroad tracks if they tumbled down the heaps in the cars. Decades later when he retired he was running the plant.

She was from Collinsville (though there was the durndest family debate because my father, for some reason, always insisted she was really from Rising Fawn, Georgia). We never heard that much about her father. Her mother took in ironing, and died young of diabetes. Much of her raising was done by her older sister and a passel of brothers. She worked during the war, and lost one of those brothers to it before marrying my father in the late 1940s.

He already had three sons—wild bucks she said she had to tame from days of running free in the darkest jungles of Woodward, Alabama. They added two more sons and a daughter.

I don't remember many days growing up when lunch wasn't three or four fresh cooked vegetables, corn bread, and a huge pitcher of iced tea. There weren't many Saturday nights when we avoided being scrubbed red and sent to bed after "Gunsmoke" because Sunday school was inescapable.

That was my parents' arc in time. They were born Southerners when the South was dirt poor. They worked hard. Feared God. And had what they had. My mother wrote that "The Old Rugged Cross" and "In the Garden" should be sung at her funeral and John 3:16 read. My father's favorite saying was an old Primitive Baptist saw: what can't be cured must be endured.

They were like hundreds of thousands of others of their generation from this state. Tough, practical, unpretentious people. They had decency in their bones. People like the group of mostly older members of the First Baptist Church of Midfield who insisted on smothering our family with food the day of my mother's funeral.

There was twenty pounds of fried chicken, every imaginable pea and bean on God's green earth, corn, breads, desserts, tea, and lots of love. When Southerners don't know what else to do for you, they cook. We're going to miss this generation when it's gone. And it's going.

The children who used to watch "Howdy Doody" are now the adults who have to make the funeral arrangements. Our parents were of the Industrial Revolution. We are of the Computer Revolution. Our arc cuts through the Shallow Age of shopping mall values and opinion poll morals. It's turning, too.

The day after the funeral, my niece Kimberly's team won the district softball championship for Helena. My ten-year-old son, Jeb, made his debut with a small part in the Summerfest production of *Oliver* two days later. Raised redneck, I keep thinking about those quarters; small circles for birth and for death. About a thought from *The Prophet* by Khalil Gibran: your children are not your children; they are the arrows you aim into the future and know not where they will land.

And about what Vicki Covington said when she visited me at the funeral home last week as we talked about the peculiarness of a mutual friend. She said it came from his not being "raised redneck." I was. I hope I can figure out how to do that for my children. I only wish my momma and daddy were here so I could tell them.

BAILEY THOMSON

A Queen for King Cotton

December 19 and 20, 1999, *Mobile Press-Register*

ALICEVILLE, Alabama—My father reached his apogee as a farmer one Indian summer day in 1956 when ten thousand sheep tumbled from the railcars at the plain, wooden Frisco Depot in our west Alabama town of Aliceville. The young animals had traveled 1,400 miles by train, from the Navajo country of New Mexico.

The October air reeked of warm lanolin—a sickly perfume—as my older brothers and the hired hands loaded the sheep into cotton wagons, the only available transport, and hauled them to our farm. The men worked until dark, while curious townspeople watched the stream of bleating captives go by.

My family kept half of the shipment, and the remaining sheep went to other farms in the area. The plan was to fatten the animals over the winter, then ship them in the spring to the New York lamb market. My father knew from having fed one thousand sheep the previous year that bad things could happen—wet weather, parasites, dogs. But at age fifty-five, he was rolling the dice in hopes that a quick profit might win for him his independence from other people's money.

Already, Bill Thomson was the biggest cotton grower in Pickens County, and usually the first to embrace innovation. Yet he wasn't satisfied. He was reminded of his dependent status each spring when he visited with the Aliceville bank's president, John A. Somerville, a dignified old gentleman whose family ranked among the local aristocracy. They would decide how much money my father needed for his crop, and Mr. John A. would advance that sum in $5,000 increments. It galled my father to gather his receipts from buying fertilizer or tractor parts and explain how he had spent the previous installment before he could draw another.

Most people around town probably thought my father had his own money. Our family lived relatively well, and although we didn't own the land we farmed, we rented some of the county's most fertile acreage. Newspapers featured my father as a model farmer, one who knew how to diversify his crops and adopt the latest technology.

In 1953, for example, a photograph in the *Tuscaloosa News* showed my father and me looking at some of the two hundred pigs he was raising. Next to us was an Alabama Cooperative Extension agent named Allen Mathews. My father had 400 acres of cotton that year, 250 acres of corn, 225 acres of soybeans, and 60 acres of grain sorghum. He told the reporter he believed in farming that reflected the latest scientific thinking—an attitude that surely pleased Mathews and his fellow Extension agents, who served as conduits between farmers and researchers at what is now Auburn University.

Sometimes, an agent would interview my father during the farm show on the little local radio station—WRAG—in nearby Carrollton. At other times, my father would speak to local groups about agriculture or some political issue. "Mr. Bill," as people always called him, tended to be the center of any conversation he joined. His careful diction and clear voice suggested he had a college education, which he didn't, and his courtly manners, especially around women, lent an air of gentility. He had a Roman nose, like his South Carolina ancestors, and blue eyes. His fair complexion forced him to cover his balding head with a hat—a straw hat in the summer and wool in the winter. He looked distinguished when dressed in a dark suit, and he favored bow ties that he knotted himself. His typical attire, however, was khaki pants and an open-neck shirt.

In 1954, my father bought a new Nash Rambler sedan in Columbus, Mississippi, about thirty miles west of Aliceville. It was white with a red top, and it had cold air blowing out of two funnels on the rear window ledge. Few people in Aliceville had seen an air-conditioned car and certainly not one with electric, push-button windows. With my mother, Attie, sitting beside him, we drove home and stopped at a little store to buy gas. An older man dressed in overalls and missing his front teeth came out to the pump, then called for his wife to come see. My father showed them how the windows worked and let the man sit at the wheel and feel the cool air blowing.

"My, my. Now ain't that nice," the man said.

"Now ain't it, though," his wife replied.

My mother, who was forty-six, could barely conceal her mirth, and we often repeated that story around the dinner table. Although my father's impetuous ideas sometimes exasperated my mother, she enjoyed being with him, and he was proud of her. She retained a trim figure and pulled her long, black hair into a bun. She loved movies and books, and she could be as passionate about politics as my father. Often, she would laugh at something he said and exclaim, "Oh, Bill, quit telling that!"

That year, in particular, they needed each other's support, because 1954 became a benchmark for hard times. Even today it haunts our family's collective memory.

By the time we bought the new Rambler, my father had planted all the cotton the federal government allowed him to grow under its price-support program. The plants grew waist high or better and were full of white blooms. There was little to do but wait and keep the boll weevils at bay. Every night after supper and a shot or two of whiskey, my father would stand on the front porch of our farmhouse and look across the fields, which began just beyond a white fence. Sometimes, the smell of fresh poison drifted across the green tops of the cotton, after a crop duster had flown over. My father would study the distant clouds for signs of moisture and measure each precious inch of rain that fell on our place. Upon arising before dawn, he would plug in the coffeepot my mother had prepared the night before and listen to WRAG for the weather report.

Around late July 1954, when I was five years old, my father loaded my mother, my brother, Matt, my sister, Becky, and me into the Rambler and headed for Panama City, Florida, and the Gulf of Mexico. We rented a seaside cabin, where my mother cooked great feasts of flounder and shrimp. My father walked the beaches to take his mind off the farm. At night we went places, even to dances at the beach pavilion. Matt was fifteen and Becky was thirteen, and it probably embarrassed them to see their father glide across the floor with a pretty girl from the crowd. My mother laughed to see him have a good time, and they often held hands.

After about a week, my brother, Tom, who was eighteen and had stayed behind, reported over the telephone that there had been no rain, and the cotton was beginning to wilt in the fierce heat. The drought had resumed. Soon, our Rambler was rolling back home. Any hope for a good crop that year had vanished like heat rays rising from a parched field.

County farmers harvested less than two hundred pounds of cotton to the acre, about half what they had expected for 1954. We kept the Nash Rambler, but my father must have come close to bankruptcy. He saved us with his ability to talk his way into another loan at the bank and more credit with the farm machinery dealers. Other big farmers were in a similar tight, but most of them owned their land and could use it as collateral. My father, by contrast, survived on his wits and his charm. He had to have money—other people's money—to make a living.

I suppose we would have been finished on the farm had the drought continued through the following year. But the weather cycle changed in 1955. The rains stayed through the summer, and the fields proved to be unusually fertile because the previous, drought-ridden crop had not sucked up all the fertilizer my father had applied. The cotton grew tall and thick. Against this deep green, the blooms luxuriated, as if the plants were ornamentals. This time, the cotton's fruit ripened into snowy balls of white fiber that averaged a bale to the acre, about five hundred pounds. On our richest fields, the yield was more than twice that average.

This time, the enemy wasn't drought but surplus. Even with the federal government's attempts to restrict acreage, impersonal forces conspired to drive down prices, as production surged in Arizona and California, where irrigated fields free of boll weevils produced bigger yields. Further competition came from synthetic fibers such as rayon. While the government struggled to prop up prices, production costs rose, as farmers resorted to bigger machinery and costly chemicals. Still, my father and other farmers in our county persisted in believing they had only to find the right combination of crops and livestock to prosper.

In fact, no other decade rivals the 1950s for the magnitude of change that swept Southern agriculture. In 1945, when one in four Alabamians depended upon farming for a livelihood, fewer than seven percent of farms had tractors. But by 1960, tractors had become so common that the agricultural census no longer enumerated mules separately. Moreover, livestock production jumped after World War II. Researchers developed new protein-rich grasses and learned how to control pests, such as flesh-eating screwworms.

Federal soil conservation programs encouraged the conversion of fields into pastures, and farmers used tractors and balers to turn hay into a profitable crop. A journalist traveling across the South in 1947 wrote that the greatest change he saw was the proliferation of beef and dairy cattle.

My father occasionally bought and sold cattle, and he often raised fine hogs. But his heart belonged to the cotton culture, in which he had been born and reared. By 1955, he was renting 1,000 acres at Vienna, a deserted town on the Tombigbee River, in addition to 350 acres where we lived, called the Bailey Place. (The name of the latter referred to the owners.) Year-round, he hired about a half-dozen tractor drivers, and during the cotton season he depended upon several large families of laborers to hoe and pick the cotton. Technology, however, was replacing even these seasonal field workers, who were becoming scarce as migration from farm to city intensified. My father bought his first mechanical cotton picker in 1955 to help harvest his bumper crop. The *Pickens County Herald* featured him in a photograph standing on the machine next to his best tractor driver, a man named "Red" Drews. Another photograph shows my father and Mr. John A., our banker, in the midst of the chest-high plants.

The picker was not as meticulous, however, as human hands. Its spindles gathered husks and other trash, which it dumped into a waiting wagon along with the cotton. The result gummed up the local gins in Aliceville, forcing my father to send his cotton about forty miles away to a farming village named Boligee, where a gin had newer equipment that could separate fiber from trash.

The burden of this responsibility harmed my father's health, I believe. By 1955, he had suffered his first heart attack, from which he never fully recovered. He had to depend even more upon his sons to help manage the farm and perform some of the skilled labor. One of my older brothers, Bo, was serving with the U.S. Army in Korea, and the next brother, Tom, had enrolled at Auburn University. Their absence left just Matthew, Becky, and me at home. Both Matt and Becky were leaders in 4-H work, and Matt was the county's top young farmer in the club's competitions. After he netted $176 an acre from his demonstration plot, the *Tuscaloosa News* declared, "Matthew has proven once again that cotton still has a place in Alabama."

My father also could count upon the local Extension agents, who frequently visited our farm and advised him how to improve his production. It was during such a conversation that he learned about feeder lambs.

In 1955, Cecil Davis, who had just come to Pickens County to be the new head agent, and his assistant, Robert Thornton, attended a seminar at the livestock experimental station at Marion Junction, a nearby crossroads. They heard a specialist named W. H. "Mutt" Gregory explain why Alabama was ideal for producing lambs for markets in the eastern United States. Gregory proposed that local farmers import thousands of the young animals in the fall, let them graze on their pastures, and then sell them in the spring, by which time the sheep would have doubled in weight. Thus Alabama would have another livestock industry, and farmers could earn cash over the otherwise idle winter months. Another incentive was that farmers could feed the corn they grew to their sheep. In 1955, corn was averaging just $1.14 per bushel, down from $1.45 the previous year. Such low grain prices were favorable for converting the corn into succulent lamb.

There were only about 12,000 sheep in the whole state, although at the turn of the century Alabama farmers reported raising more than 300,000 head. In fact, production for the United States had fallen from fifty-one million head in 1884 to just twenty-six million. Some said the military cooks' clumsy attempts to serve mutton during World War II turned GIs' stomachs. More certain were the ravages from internal parasites that infested Southern flocks.

But if Alabamians shunned the meat, many big-city neighborhoods, especially along the East Coast, retained their taste for lamb. Auburn's Gregory assured Extension agents that sheep were the most profitable livestock, and that science could control the pests. Indeed, sheep were the only animals that could fatten out to market weight—at least, theoretically—on grass alone.

Gregory worked with a buying agent for Armour and Company named E. H. Mattingly of St. Louis. Armour was eager to develop a lamb supply east of the Mississippi River, and especially one that could compete with areas such as Virginia that traditionally produced eastern spring lamb. The plan for 1955 called for Alabama farmers to import about fifty thousand feeder lambs from Arizona and New Mexico, where the Navajo and Hopi Indians raised huge flocks. Armour offered to lend growers money to pay for the stock at four percent interest. The company guaranteed it would buy the lambs back in the spring and pay the farmers for the weight that the animals gained.

The idea attracted farmers in forty-nine of Alabama's sixty-seven counties. In Pickens County, Davis promoted the idea over his weekly radio show. Ten farmers responded and put down $100 each toward the first shipment in October. They also agreed to pay for vaccinations. My father signed up for one thousand head. Under the agreement, the farmers could keep up to half of the females— the ewes—to build a permanent flock. In announcing the new program, the Cooperative Extension Service declared, "This potential with sheep for the years ahead looks like one of the safest and best on many farms in Alabama."

The sheep bound for Pickens arrived one crisp football afternoon in October at the Frisco Depot in Aliceville. Davis and Thornton were there to help unload the animals, but there was trouble. The lambs arrived about three weeks later than expected, and many had lost weight. Farmers looked through the slats of the livestock cars, shook their heads, and even cursed the venture. They had been charged for fifty-pound lambs, but many of the animals weighed only half that. My father, however, didn't pay much attention to such discouraging details. He was ready to get on with raising sheep. His helpers hauled the sheep back to the Bailey Place, where we had a large livestock barn and good pastures.

Until that fall of 1955, my father's only association with sheep came from Bible stories he had learned as a child. Still, he probably figured that sheep acted pretty much as cows and hogs did. Therefore, if one simply went behind the animals, whooping and waving one's arms, they would move in unison toward the desired destination.

Actually, herding sheep is like pushing Jell-O. You can get some of them going on one end of the flock, but cooperation sags at the other end.

One afternoon, as the sheep milled around on our place, my father decided to herd them to the barn lot, where we fed them grain at night and protected them from predators. He began waving his arms and hollering. The sheep looked at him with their unknowing eyes and marched around in circles. My father resorted to more exaggerated motions and yelling, while beginning to run behind the frightened creatures. He even tried baaing like a sheep. Suddenly, his feet went out from under him and he landed on his back. His unrepentant flock stared dumbly at his predicament.

Such frustration persuaded my father that the farm needed a herding dog. Two dogs, in fact. He found them by word of mouth, I suppose, and we picked them up at the owner's country store. They were rough collies, along the Lassie model, and their beautiful looks suggested that they were supposed to herd something. My father introduced them to their new charges, and the dogs looked back at him with uncertainty. We might just as well have taken our bird dogs to the pasture, for all the good Lassie's look-alikes did. Within a few weeks, my father hauled the dogs back. A year would pass before we realized that the proper herding dog for sheep was not the beautiful rough collie but rather its lean, working-class cousin, the Border collie.

Gradually, we learned more about our flock and how to care for it. Every morning, the sheep would walk out through a fenced passage to the big grazing area about a quarter of a mile from the barn. One of the hands would check on them during the day, and in the evening several of us would bring them back. Walking behind the animals with my brothers and the hands, I learned how to get a few of the sheep started in the right direction and then encourage the rest to follow. There were no days off from this routine, unlike cultivating cotton, which allowed the crew to knock off at dinnertime on Saturday.

One reward for this hard work, however, occurred after about half a dozen of the lambs fattened too early for the market. My father had them slaughtered, and my mother learned to cook leg of lamb and extra-thick chops. As my father's partner, she did not busy herself with many details of the farm. She preferred to run our large household, cooking fresh vegetables, meats, and cornbread for the noon-day meal that she served seven days a week to her family and to any farmhands lucky enough to be around. Her life outside the home centered on the church—singing in the choir, teaching Sunday school, and attending circle meetings.

In early March, Armour arranged for a crew to shear our sheep. They worked in the barn with their electric shears, while my brother Matt and other hands chased down sheep for them. These shearers, who had a strange accent that probably was Australian, could yank an animal up like a small child and have its fleece off in a minute or less. Our hired hands swept the wool into piles, then threw it into sacks six or eight feet long hanging from scaffolds. A worker named Tyler, who seemed enormous to me, yet gentle and meek, climbed into the sacks and trampled the wool into a compact mass.

Despite our inexperience, the sheep experiment went remarkably well, at least for our farm. One reason was that my father followed the county agents' instructions. To control the parasites, the main one being a stomach worm, we treated the lambs with a dose of nicotine and copper sulfate, which was a common remedy in the 1950s. There was enough grass to fatten them, with a supplement of some ground corn, and the lambs reached eighty pounds or more by springtime.

According to the *Pickens County Herald,* my father was the first to ship a railcar load of feeder lambs from Alabama. That was in March 1956. A few weeks later, eight more carloads left the county, accompanied by two from Tuscaloosa. Under the agreement with Armour, farmers received the same price for their lambs that the St. Louis markets offered on that particular marketing day, which came to about nineteen cents a pound.

The *Herald* quoted Agent Thornton as the lambs were being loaded: "A new day may be dawning for the raising and feeding of sheep in this county." Our father certainly thought so. Our farm made enough money on the first sheep to suggest that he had found a queen for King Cotton—a fat feeder lamb. Next time, he would cut his own deal with Armour and raise the stakes fivefold.

Part Two: Winter of Rains and Ruin

My brother Bo returned home to our farm in March 1956, having finished his tour with the U.S. Army as a military policeman in Korea. I remember, as a first-grader, rushing from the school bus and leaping into his arms. He was still wearing his olive-green fatigues.

Bo was twenty-six, weighed about 160 pounds, and stood six feet tall. Like my father, Bill Thomson, he had a fair complexion and handsome looks. The two men also shared an enthusiasm for trying new ventures on our cotton farm, which was a good thing, because we had imported one thousand feeder lambs from New Mexico that winter to boost our income. After fattening the young sheep, we sold them in the spring to Armour and Company and realized a nice profit. My father had a mind that we would raise many thousands more lambs the following fall.

Bo came home expecting to be my father's junior partner on the farm. But their different temperaments set them apart. Bo liked mechanical things, and his preference for precision carried over to his personality. He wanted jobs done correctly and for rational reasons. His military service had exposed him to a different management style from the casual way my father ran the farm. However tiresome Army life might have been, Bo could count on other people carrying out their jobs according to clear rules.

Not so when "Mr. Bill" was in charge. His way was paternalistic and personal. He didn't consult with anyone when he wanted to change things, save perhaps his banker, Mr. John A. Somerville, from whom he secured a large loan each year to make his cotton crop—the biggest in Pickens County. He had no formal system for keeping records, other than his canceled checks. Every Saturday afternoon, he dispensed pay and wisdom to his tractor drivers and other workers, often meeting with them under a shade tree behind the house. Other times, he entertained his friends around our dinner table. Most of them were cotton growers like him, drawn by his spirited conversation and his bourbon toddies in the late afternoons.

I might add that my mother understood both of her men and sometimes mediated differences between father and son. She kept a stable, dignified home, counterbalancing my father's penchant for adventure and risk. Unlike him, she was deeply religious, calling on God and the Methodist Church to help raise her children and see us through difficult times on the farm. She did not interfere in the management, but her wise counsel and inner strength were assets as valuable as my father's creative mind and my brother's mechanical competency.

With his fatigues and his photographs of Korea tucked away in a bottom drawer, Bo assumed the major duties of planting and harvesting the cotton crop in 1956. As the bolls ripened and burst open, he kept the cotton picker and other machinery running. He also supervised the field hands, usually forty or more at a time. Some lived at Panola, a farming hamlet about twenty miles away. Bo would crank our big flatbed truck before dawn to fetch them and then head to our cotton fields.

During the cotton-picking season, he would weigh their day's work in the late afternoon, using a scale that hung from a two-by-four nailed to a wagon. Bo would call out the amount to be credited to that particular picker's family, and one of our regular hands would record the numbers. Often one or two young African American women in their late teens would keep an independent tally of weights. I don't know how much schooling they had, for their families depended upon them to work during the hoeing and picking seasons.

After Bo returned to be, in effect, the farm's foreman, my father could relax a little more. We took a trip down to the beach, to Panama City, Florida, that summer; then in September, my brother Tom left to attend college at Auburn University, about two hundred miles to the east, and my other brother Matt began his senior year in high school as captain of Aliceville's football team. Sometimes, my father would pick Matt up before practice ended so he could help with the chores. The late summer mellowed into a pleasant fall that brought success on the football field and the farm. Matt made the all-county team, and our farm turned a nice profit for 1956.

It was about that time that my father resolved to parlay our cotton earnings into a bigger stake—one that might free us from borrowing and even allow us to quit renting land and start buying it. He negotiated with Armour and Company, agreeing to import ten thousand feeder lambs from New Mexico, half of which he would distribute to several subcontractors and half of which he would raise himself through the winter of 1956–57. Armour agreed to buy the lambs from us the following spring once they had nearly doubled their weight.

The company had its eye on consumers in New York and other Eastern cities who relished fresh lamb. Southern producers such as my father were closer to those consumers than were the ranches out West and could presumably get their sheep there quicker, especially for the finicky kosher markets, which had strict rules about slaughtering livestock. Also, lambs could reach their prime quicker by grazing on Southern winter pastures—or at least that was the theory that Armour's agents promoted.

The company invited my father to fly to Gallup, New Mexico, aboard commercial airliners and spend a week selecting his sheep from the huge flocks of Rambouillet lambs the Navajo Indians offered to sell. He sent us postcards of Indians, which showed them living in huts called hogans and tending their sheep. When he returned, he had on a new Stetson hat, and he wore a string tie with a figurine made by a Navajo craftsman. I remember how good and confident he looked that fall.

As the ten thousand sheep arrived at Aliceville's Frisco Depot that October day in 1956, I suspect, a lot of people admired my father's ambition, even as others expressed skepticism about all the wagons full of woollies passing through town. Some folks compared this exotic event to the arrival of German prisoners of war in 1943, after the Army built a camp just outside of town. The POWs, who were captured from Erwin Rommel's Afrika Korps, had disembarked at that same depot and marched to barracks ringed by barbed wire.

Aliceville had enjoyed a boom from the Army's payroll for camp workers and guards. The town also benefited from the American soldiers who returned home after the war and became leaders and boosters. They were more ambitious for Aliceville than their parents had been. These young men joined the Chamber of Commerce and the local civic clubs and liked to say Aliceville was the "Biggest Little Town in West Alabama." In 1953, when Aliceville had about 3,500 people, the city council installed parking meters and the Post Office began home mail delivery. Three years later, Aliceville persuaded a company called F. C. Huyck and Sons of New York to build a plant for making industrial felts. The town already had a cotton mill, founded in 1928, which had ten thousand spindles and a village where many of its workers lived.

My father's adventuresome style complemented the town's rising confidence. He belonged to a new era of farming that bore only a superficial resemblance to the old plantations. By now, most of the poor sharecroppers had disappeared from Southern agriculture, and commercial farmers like my father combined heavy capital investment with scientific methods to produce larger crops. They depended largely upon machines such as big tractors and cotton pickers. They were also quicker to diversify production than their predecessors had been.

While my father enjoyed surprising the townspeople with his second shipment of young sheep, my brother Bo's perspective was quite different. The responsibility for tending the five thousand fell upon him.

No sooner had Bo and the hands settled the sheep into their new home, at our farm known as the Bailey Place, than rains began. Over the next months, the feedlot and pastures turned into deep mud from thousands of churning hooves.

Bo had to send part of the flock to our other place, a farm at Vienna, a ghost town about five miles away. He allowed some of the sheep to forage over harvested cornfields—any place that could provide room and fodder. Fog often followed the rains, throwing a damp shroud over the sheep as Bo arrived each morning to tend them. The Tombigbee River bounded the place, and its waters rose over some of the pastures. To escape the flood, one bunch of sheep crawled out on a fallen tree, like birds on a telephone wire. The next morning, they forlornly greeted Bo and Robert Thornton, the assistant county agent.

That fall, Bo met an attractive young woman named Nancy Herron, who came from Mississippi to teach commercial classes at the high school. They began courting, but Bo's farm work often interfered with romance. He usually didn't get home until after dark, and then he couldn't seem to scrape all the manure from his boots. Sometimes, it was too late to attend the picture show; so the young couple just rode down to Vienna for Bo to check on the sheep one more time—at least that was his excuse to be alone with Nancy.

As pasture grass disappeared, my father decided to feed the sheep corn we had grown that year. The animals, however, were finicky eaters and often regurgitated the grain unless Bo had it ground into meal. Mud from all the rain prevented him from hauling the feed into the pastures. Instead, he and his helpers had to carry the feed sacks by hand from the road to the troughs, wading through the muck as they went. To improve the grazing, they planted winter grass. One January day, it was so cold that Matt developed an earache while putting out soda to stimulate the grass's growth. His ailment turned into Bell's palsy, leaving one side of his face paralyzed. He suffered from the affliction for two months, and some of his high school annual pictures reveal his distorted face.

The sheep began coming down with various ailments themselves, including pneumonia and stomach worms. They probably had these parasites when they arrived from New Mexico. The worms would proliferate by laying eggs, which the sheep would excrete with its feces. The worms would hatch and crawl on the grass, and another sheep would eat them, passing on the infection. In Navajo country, the worms often died in the dry land, so they weren't such a problem there. My brothers took to dosing the animals, poking metal tubes down their throats or using glass bottles with long necks to inject the medicine.

Bo built a fenced runway that allowed him to separate the sick sheep from the others, but he couldn't stop the dying. Carcasses lay on the ground every new morning.

The final blow that winter arrived with the bone-chilling howl of a dog.

The Navajos had learned their herding from the early Spanish settlers, who introduced sheep into the Southwest. A sheep-raising culture developed along both sides of what is now the U.S.–Mexican border, and it encouraged a semi-nomadic life, as shepherds moved their flocks back and forth with the seasons. Sheep bred for this kind of existence were tough survivors, but only within their native environment. They never faced wet winters. Nor were they accustomed to living in more settled areas, where neighbors' dogs formed into vicious packs.

Pastures at Vienna, with its one thousand acres, were isolated and surrounded by woods. Many families who worked on the farms still lived near the old river settlement, and virtually all of them kept dogs for hunting. Most were skinny, cowering animals that seemed harmless. But gathered in packs, they turned into marauding killers, emerging from the woods to run the sheep until the poor creatures expired from fear and exhaustion.

Once the dogs had tasted blood, there would be no respite.

As the losses climbed into the hundreds, Bo went around and asked the families to pen their dogs. But confinement was unknown in those days. Bo's frustration boiled over. He took to carrying a twelve-gauge shotgun, and he and Matt and sometimes our brother Tom, when he was home from Auburn, took turns guarding the sheep after dark. I spent several nights with them, curled up in a blanket inside our Nash Rambler automobile.

One morning, Bo stopped to talk to some neighbors who were walking by one of our pastures. A dog appeared under the barbed-wire fence and began to stalk some of the sheep. Bo retrieved his gun from the pickup and dropped to one knee with military precision. He killed the dog with a single shot. Word quickly spread through the community after the episode that Bo meant what he said about keeping dogs away from our sheep. Gradually, the threat subsided.

Even as he felt cursed by these local killers, Bo discovered that a Border collie could be the herdsman's right arm. A man in town had such a collie, but she wouldn't mind him. He offered her to Bo, and almost immediately a partnership formed between man and dog.

Lady, as we named her, was used to herding cattle, but she adapted quickly to the sheep. To retrieve a flock from a pasture, Bo would send her in a broad semicircle, and she would work her way back with the sheep in front of her. The dog's ability astonished us. A Border collie has an innate desire to chase down prey. Sheep, being descendants of hunted animals, understand the dog's intentions and try to stay out of its way. The result is a controlled panic, with the dog mesmerizing the sheep with its eyes while curbing its instinct to kill. A single herder and a trained Border collie can handle a pasture full of animals, bringing them to the barn, cutting out individuals that need attention and pushing the whole bunch into holding pens or onto trucks.

We always spoke of Lady as the smartest dog we had ever seen. She rode everywhere in the truck with Bo, and sometimes he stopped to let her herd chickens or cows for the fun of it. Afterward, she loved to cool off in a puddle of water or a drinking trough, forcing Bo to put her in the back of the truck for the rest of the ride. When her day was done, Lady stayed in the yard, sleeping under the porch, never mixing with our hunting dogs. She would tolerate no roughhousing from me, and once she ran off when I decided, impetuously, that she needed a bath. Lady lived to work, and she had plenty of opportunities as the No. 1 hand around the sheep. After her arrival, we had no more problems making the animals go where we wished.

I became a proficient herder myself, although I was only eight. My father would send me into the pasture, and I would return with the flock, as Lady made her worried rounds from one side to the other. Other times, I went with my brothers to feed the sheep or to watch them dose the animals with medicine. Pictures that Bo took with his 35 mm camera show me in the pastures or posing behind the Border collie, with sheep in the background. Work was play for me. When some small job came my way, I took pleasure from pretending it was serious, much as I played out endless B-grade movies in my head about cowboys or Civil War soldiers.

As the rains finally diminished and jonquils began pushing up to the warming sun, my father grew anxious to get his sheep to market—that is, those that had survived that terrible winter. To qualify as prime or choice grades in the lamb markets, the ideal carcass in those days required about two- to three-tenths of an inch of fat around it. Graders would run their hands along the animals' backs to feel the fat along the ribs.

To my father's great disappointment, less than five percent of our sheep had put on enough fat that winter to earn the highest prices. He couldn't understand this poor performance, and Armour's agents seemed equally puzzled. We had fed the sheep all the corn we had grown in 1956, although they were supposed to have fattened on pastures alone. We even imported grain from the Midwest, once ours ran out.

Along with the corn vanished any hopes for a profit. I don't know if anyone, besides my mother and our banker, ever heard my father say how much money he lost. He wasn't one to dwell on failure. But clearly the biggest deficit from our venture was the hundreds of man-hours that my brothers Bo and Matt invested during that terrible winter—even on Sundays—out in the cold, wet fields, only to realize no reward for the family that spring. It added up to rotten economics, a condition farmers have endured for ages.

Many years later, I learned from a specialist at Mississippi State University that the Navajo Rambouillet sheep were notoriously slow to gain weight. Farmers in Mississippi who also were experimenting with lambs during the 1950s had better luck with animals imported from Texas.

We did have one nice surprise after the shearing men showed up at our farm to strip the thick fleeces from the lambs. We received a fat federal subsidy for the wool. It was a typical gesture from the '50s: a federal check to keep farmers just ahead of disaster.

By this time, my father's enthusiasm and Bo's energy were exhausted. They sent the sheep away in the same fashion as the animals had arrived at our farm, in cotton wagons with high rails and on the back of our big flatbed truck.

When the last of the lambs were shipped north and my father was back to planting cotton, which he knew best, someone in town asked him what he thought about his adventure, now that it was over. "I just wish all those damned sheep had died with Moses," he replied. "We would have been a lot better off."

The failure of the sheep venture did not mean that my father quit trying new things. Soon, he and other farmers in the county were producing cucumbers as a side crop to sell to a Montgomery pickle outfit. The scale was nothing like that of the sheep project, but the experiment attracted attention. The *Pickens County Herald* again featured my father as a smart farmer who knew how to diversify his crops.

Bo left the farmers' ranks soon after the sheep venture ended. He married Nancy in the summer of 1957, and they lived at the Bailey Place after my parents had moved the rest of us back to a house we owned in town. We had a large cotton crop that fall, but the next spring my father lost half of his allotment when the government again reduced acreage, hoping to curb production and boost prices. Two families couldn't live on just two hundred acres of cotton, so Bo got a job at the new Huyck plant seven miles south of Aliceville.

Ironically, the plant, which had headquarters in Rensselaer, New York, was one of the nation's largest consumers of wool, which it used in making its industrial felts. In September 1956, a representative of Huyck had urged local farmers like my father to produce wool for the plant, but he warned: "There are hazards to sheep-raising. Farmers need to know this." Two years later, the plant had in my brother Bo an employee who could offer personal testimony.

Factory work wasn't something that suited Bo, who as my father's foreman had run a large farm and supervised dozens of workers. He surprised everyone, except Nancy, when he enrolled at Mississippi State over at Starkville, about fifty miles away. He completed the engineering program on the GI Bill, taking no summers off. He often studied so hard he developed migraine-like headaches that spread into his shoulders. But no challenge at Mississippi State came close to what he endured during that awful winter of the sheep.

My father continued to farm for a few more years. My brother Matt, who by this time was studying business at The University of Alabama, an hour away in Tuscaloosa, worked with him on weekends and during the summers. My sister, Becky, departed for Mississippi State College for Women in nearby Columbus in 1959, leaving me at home as the last child. By this time, I had moved up to driving a small tractor that we used for odd jobs, such as pulling a wagon loaded with fertilizer and seed during planting season. I also stood on a wooden plank behind the hoppers of the four-row planter to make sure seed and fertilizer fell into the ground properly.

One afternoon in April 1961 my father suffered a stroke while he was out in the fields. Several of the hired hands gathered him into the big truck and sped to our house in town. I was at home, working in the garden, which I cultivated as a 4-H project. A friend was helping me, and we watched the truck pull into the gravel driveway. One of the hands ran to summon my mother. She had the men transfer my stricken father to our car and then drove him to the hospital there in Aliceville.

Matt came home from the university to run the farm until we harvested the cotton that fall. My father got better, but he never regained his health sufficiently to grow cotton again. We had made our last crop. My father subleased his fields and sold his equipment, although we did raise several hundred hogs at the Bailey Place for a year or so after that. And my brothers and I continued to hunt over the land, enjoying one of the few privileges of the farming class. One day in the woods we came across the bones of a ram that had somehow escaped from the pasture and taken a few ewes with him during the sheep-raising days.

My father died of cancer in August 1963, when I was fourteen. The Methodist church was full of mourners. At the cemetery, I noticed a small knot of men standing off to one side. They were his former tractor hands, come to pay their respects.

Loblolly pine trees now cover the old cotton fields around Aliceville. Only about three cotton farmers remain in all of Pickens County, compared with the 1,800 who reported growing cotton in 1954. At that time, eleven gins hummed with business in the county. None of them survives, nor does the Huyck plant, which closed a few years ago after a corporate shakeup.

One of the last cotton farmers is Hugh Summerville. He is president of Cotton Inc., a national group that collects dues from farmers to promote the fiber. But Summerville and his colleagues have not resolved the problem that haunted my father's generation: cheaper prices from global competition.

A local man, Everett Owens, cultivates part of the old Vienna place where we once grew cotton and grazed our sheep along the banks of the Tombigbee. Owens produces sod for suburban lawns. I wonder what my father would think if he could see his fields covered with sod, after he had spent so much money and energy trying to keep Johnson grass and nut grass from his cotton.

I moved close to my old home in 1996 to teach journalism at The University of Alabama, after spending twenty-five years in newspapering. That was the last year of my mother's life. I often asked her about our farming days and my father's willingness to take a risk. She still spoke of him with an abiding love, but once she said, with a bit of frustration, "Your father would never stay with anything long enough." But I don't think she had sheep in mind when she said that.

Farming was what my father knew and what he loved. He hoped each year that his fortunes would improve, and he looked for new ways to make that happen. Our sheep venture was simply one more thing to try, and when that didn't work he went on to the next. Until the end, he remained defiant of debt, bad weather, and even poor health.

He left us with a good name, which the Bible says is preferable to great riches.

Index